Picture Postcards

from

France & Belgium

1914 - 1925

The Collection of

Private Thomas Wainwright,

34360, RAMC

Edited by

Lyn Dyson

Private Thomas Wainwright

Tom was born in Ludlow, Shropshire in 1887, the son of Thomas Wainwright, a saddler, and his wife Anne Bengry. Tom grew up in a large family with three brothers, one of whom died in infancy, and nine sisters. His other brother was killed in a cycle accident in 1903, so when war broke out in 1914, Tom was the only surviving son of Thomas and Anne Wainwright.

In 1914 Tom was working in his father's saddlery and leather shop at 1 Bull Ring, Ludlow. His father was apparently a hard task master, and this may have been one of the reasons Tom was so quick to enlist when the call was made for volunteers.

He enlisted on 4th September 1914 and arrived in camp at Aldershot on 6th September. The men were asked whether anyone had any first aid experience, and Tom admitted that he had. He was therefore allocated to the Royal Army Medical Corps.

He became a nursing orderly and served almost the entire war at the British Red Cross Base Hospital at Wimereux in Normandy. In 1917 no fewer than ten hospitals were operating in Wimereux to care for the wounded and sick soldiers returning from the Western Front. They dealt with the wounded from the Ypres-Armentieres-Arras sectors. Those who succumbed to their wounds were buried in the town's cemetery; however by 1918 a lack of available space meant that a new cemetery was opened in nearby Wimille, the Terlincthun British Cemetery.

During his days off duty, Tom would explore the area surrounding the hospital, walking for miles, choosing various locations to sit down and write home. His letters have been published in a book entitled "Uncle Tom's Letters."

Tom's sister, my grandmother Annie Wainwright, was an avid postcard collector, and Tom sent postcards regularly to her and to his other sisters. Along the way he also started his own collection, and this forms the base of this book.

Most of the postcards were printed before the war, and they give us a glimpse of life in France at that time. I guess it was never the same afterwards.

Tom remained in Wimereux until August 1918 when he was posted to 46th Field Ambulance, attached to the 15th Scottish Regiment with the First Army. He was involved in the Final Advance on Artois from 2nd October 1918 to the Armistice.

Tom was de-mobilized on 22nd February 1919, having spent the last couple of months in Belgium.

On his return to civilian life in 1919 Tom resumed his position in his father's business, eventually inheriting it.

He did return to France and Belgium in 1924/1925, and one or two of the postcards are from that visit.

Tom died in Ludlow in 1989, at the age of 101. He never married, but has an extensive family of nephews, nieces, great nephews and nieces, and great great nephews and nieces.

Lyn Dyson December 2014

Private Thomas Wainwright, 34360, RAMC

France

Abbeville

Abbeville is situated on the River Somme

5 ABBEVILLE. — *Panorama sur l'Hôpital.* — LL.

CARTE POSTALE

CORRESPONDANCE	ADRESSE

On our way to Boulogne we were delayed here a day, owing to an accident on the line further on. Was unable to get into the town.

Since then the Germans have dropped bombs on Abbeville.

Ambleteuse

This village was about 3.5 miles from the Hospital. This card was sent in April 1918

At the end of the 19th century Ambleteuse became a popular place for holidays for people from Lille and Paris.

E. S. 1616. AMBLETEUSE (P.-de-C.) — L'Église et le Centre

E. S. 1631. AMBLETEUSE (P.-de-C.) — Parc et Tennis

Sent April 1918

This Napoleonic fort was described as in a better state of preservation than others Tom had seen.

Baincthun

Tom said that not many soldiers made it to the out of the way villages, and he was often stared at as he walked through.

This postcard was purchased at the café outside which the people were standing. Tom climbed to the top of the hill in the background, which he described as an Angel Bank. It took him fifteen minutes to climb it.

Environs de Boulogne-sur-Mer. - BAINCTHUN. - Le Calvaire

Sent in April 1918

Baincthun was a farming and quarrying community situated four miles southeast of Boulogne.

Boulogne sur Mer

Stévenard, édit., Boulogne-sur-Mer.

95 · BOULOGNE-SUR-MER. — Sur la Plage. — LL.

BOULOGNE-SUR-MER. — Le Casino

L. D., B., 270
Environs de Boulogne-sur-Mer
Le Hameau de la Poterie

BOULOGNE-SUR-MER. — Le Quai Gambetta. — LL.

88 BOULOGNE SUR-MER. — Le Casino et les Jetees. — LL.

Gris - Nez

1 AU CAP GRIS-NEZ. — La Plage. — LL.

Édition de la Librairie Lorenza

E. S. 2009. GRIS-NEZ (P.-de-C.) — Le Carrefour

Stevenard, édit. Boulogne-sur-Mer

Hardelot

1 HARDELOT-PLAGE. — L'Hostellerie des Marmousets. — LL.

10 LE CHÂTEAU D'HARDELOT. — Les Remparts (Côté Est). — LL.

L. D., B., 292. - Environs de Boulogne-sur-Mer. - Le Château d'Hardelot

(Emplacement d'un Château fort restauré en 1232
par Hurepel, comte de Boulogne, habité par Henri VIII
d'Angleterre et détruit en 1668 par de Campaigne.)

Le Havre

66. LE HAVRE — *Panorama, pris de la Héve*

161. LE HAVRE — *Panorama, pris de l'Hôtel-de-Ville*

19

Le Portel

Le Portel is a fishing town situated about two miles southwest of Boulogne.

27 LE PORTEL. — La Plage et le Vieux Fort. — LL.

33 LE PORTEL. — Le Port et la Plage. — LL.

21

E. S. 781. - Environs
de Boulogne - sur - Mer
LE PORTEL
Sortie de l'Église
pour la Procession

Stévenard, édit., Boulogne-sur-Mer

E. S. 777. Environs de Boulogne-sur-Mer - LE PORTEL
Type de Matelots Perteloise

Licques

Licques is a farming village located about 15 miles south of Calais.

LICQUES (P.-de-C.). - Vue panoramique, prise du haut du Vignot

Marquise

Marquise is a farming and quarrying community situated about 10 miles northeast of Boulogne.

Stévenard, édit., Boulogne-sur-Mer

E S. 2336. MARQUISE (P.-de-C.)
Intérieur de l'Eglise

Stevenard, édit. Boulogne-sur-Mer

E. S. 2348. MARQUISE (P.-de-C) — Rue de l'Eglise

Paris

1028 — PARIS.
La Tour Eiffel, vue prise du Trocadéro.   Eiffel Tower, view taken from Trocadéro.

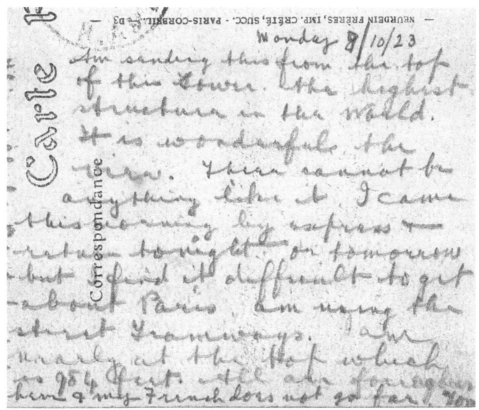

This card was sent in July 1918, and Tom was still expecting to be sent to Field Ambulance. He said he was often hungry as most of his work was out of doors, and the meals were often unsatisfying. However he was feeling very fit.

Rouen

1 — ROUEN   Vue générale, prise de Bon-Secours.   ND. Phot.

Sainte-Adresse

Sainte-Adresse is situated two miles northwest of Le Havre

197.   SAINTE-ADRESSE — Rue du Beau Panorama

Souverain-Moulin

1 — ENVIRONS DE BOULOGNE-SUR-MER — SOUVERAIN-MOULIN
Le gué de Cuverville, emplacement d'un pont défendu par PATRAS-DE-CAMPAIGNO
contre les Espagnols en 1595 ; l'héroïque gouverneur de Boulogne y trouva la mort

Tom often walked to this village

ENVIRONS DE BOULOGNE-SUR-MER ET WIMEREUX
SOUVERAIN-MOULIN — Le Pont

At the end of the road the café can be seen

26 – SOUVERAIN-MOULIN. – L'Église

L. D. B. 664. - Environs de Boulogne-s/-Mer
SOUVERAIN-MOULIN. - Le marché aux chevaux

ENVIRONS DE BOULOGNE-SUR-MER ET WIMEREUX
SOUVERAIN-MOULIN. – La foire du 25 Août

Cliché Octave LELARD

Wimereux

:96 WIMEREUX. — *Vue prise de la Falaise nord.* — LL.

The cross indicates where Tom would often sit and write home. He said it wasn't as steep as it looks in the photograph!

45   WIMEREUX. — Vue prise du Casino. — LL.

59 WIMEREUX. — Là Rue St-Armand. — LL.

L. D., B., 695. - WIMEREUX. - Le Temple Anglais
(The Christ Church - Church of England)

7 WIMEREUX. — Le Grand Hôtel et la Plage. — LL.

L. D., B., 247. - WIMEREUX
Le Calvaire

326. Environs de BOULOGNE-sur-MER
Wilmereux - Rue Carnot
et Hôtel Continental

L'Hirondelle, Paris

46 WIMEREUX. — Vue panoramique prise des Dunes. — LL.

Édition de la Librairie Douchy-Lorenza

42. WIMEREUX. — Le Nouveau Casino. — LL.

Wimereux

Enfants jouant sur la Plage

LL.

Wimereux

La Plage et les Châlets

LL

E. S. 1410. WIMEREUX (P.-de-C.)
Carrefour de la Rue Carnot

Stévenard, édit., Boulogne-sur-Mer

E. S. 1405. WIMEREUX (P.-de-C.) - Le Casino.

41 WIMEREUX. — Le Casino pris de la Plage — LL.

Édition de la Librairie Douchy-Lorenza

10 WIMEREUX. — Vue generale de la Plage. — LL.

Edition de la Librairie Douchy-Lorenza

The Hotel Splendid is on the left of this picture, and was the Officer's Hospital during the war.

WIMEREUX-CIMETRY. — Graves of the British and Colonial Army.

Sent September 1925

Wimille

Wimille is a farming and light industry town situated three miles nth of Boulogne

Stevenard, édit. Boulogne-sur-Mer

E. S. 1555 WIMILLE (P.-de-C.)

Monument élevé à la mémoire de Pilâtre de Rosier et de Pierre Romain,
Aéronautes tombés de ballon le 17 Juin 1764, Cimetière de Wimille

WIMILLE (P.-de-C.)
Entrée de Wimille par la Route de Boulogne
E. S. 27-6

Wissant

Wissant is a fishing port situated 11 miles north of Boulogne

The Mairie is to the left of the church

E. S. 2221. WISSANT (P.-de-C.) — Vue de Villas

Tom described this as a deserted sort of place, with all the big houses lying empty.

Belgium

Ath

ATH — Panorama No 2.

Beloeil

Beloeil — Le Pont d'entrée du Château

The lake was alive with fish. This was the residence of a Belgian prince before the war, and was described as a very grand place.

This town was about twenty minutes' walk from Tom's billet. He listened to the band playing behind the statue.

BELOEIL. — Le Bassin de Neptune
dans le Parc du Château

Bruxelles

Bruxelles - La Grand'Place
Côté Sud-Ouest : L'Hôtel de Ville.

Bruxelles Eglise Sainte-Gudule.

Huissignies

HUISSIGNIES. Le Chemin du Moulin.

Edit. Equeter-Lorphevre

HUISSIGNIES. La Rue de la Gare.

CAFE DE LA GARE
E ROUSSEAU DATH

Edit. Equeter-Lorphevre

Nivelles

Nivelles — Collégiale Ste-Gertrude, (1046)
A l'avant plan : nef principale, comprenant 8 travées. Autrefois couverte d'un plafond, elle a été voûtée en 1650 par l'abbesse de Lannoy. La corniche et la décoration des piliers datant de 1745 et le pavement de 1772 sont dus à l'initiative des chanoines Le Hoye. Dans le fond : Le croisillon et le chœur qui viennent d'être dépouillés de leur revêtement Louis XV (1753) et rétablis dans leurs lignes primitives, sous la direction de M. A. Verhaegen.
E. Desaix, éditeur, Bruxelles. — Reprod. interd.

Tom was billeted about 300 yards from the church

NIVELLES   Grand'Place et le Kiosque

On the left is the church, with houses built up against it. The Recreation room for the troops was just below where the man and two children are walking. The Scottish pipers and buglers marched up and down the road every day at 4pm.

Tournai

TOURNAI. — LE BEFFROI.

On his way back from leave in December 1918, Tom stayed here and listened to a British band playing under the tree.

Waterloo

Waterloo — Panorama de la plaine de Waterloo. Vue sur Waterloo et Mont St. Jean.
Panorama of the battlefield of Waterloo and Mont St. Jean.

Waterloo
La Butte et le Lion

La Butte a 45 mètres de hauteur, et l'on arrive au sommet par 226 marches. Le Lion qui la surmonte a été fondu par Cockerill avec le bronze des canons pris par les Alliés.

In Memory of Waterloo.
Panorama of the Battle-Field.

The Belgians, willingly embracing the opportunity of destroying the french domination, united with the Dutchmen under the Prince of Orange and took part in the battle of the 18th June 1815, where the army of Napoleon was defeated by the English troops under Wellington and the Germans under Blücher. Near the farm the French have erected a monument in memory of their comrades who died in this battle.

Waterloo   Vue intérieure d'Hougoumont. La ferme, la chapelle et le puits aux cadavres.

11. *Panorama van den slag van Waterloo*

De brigade Nederlandsche Kavalerie van Ghigny snelt de carré's te hulp. Tusschen de rook zien wij een generaal, die door een pistoolschot getroffen, op zijn paard in een zakt. Het is de belgische Generaal Van Merlen, Kommandant van de 2de brigade der lichte nederlandsche Kavalerie, die eenige oogenblikken daarna door een kanonskogel werd gedood. Meer naar rechtsch dan Van Merlen, staat de engelsche opperbevelhebber Hertog van Wellington, kalm en onverzettelijk. Nog meer naar rechts de Prins van Oranje, die gekwetst werd op de plaats waar het panorama staat, op het oogenblik waarop de moyenne garde tusschen bieden kwam.

Ypres

50618-1. — Ypres. Les Halles aux draps en 1919   *The Clothiers' Halles in 1919.*

Sent in October 1925

Miscellaneous Postcards

This card was sent on April 1st 1918 and Tom was engaged in stretcher bearing as the wounded were brought to the hospital. Most of the A fit men were sent to field ambulance duty at this time, and Tom was in daily expectation of joining them. He said he was fit and ready for anything.

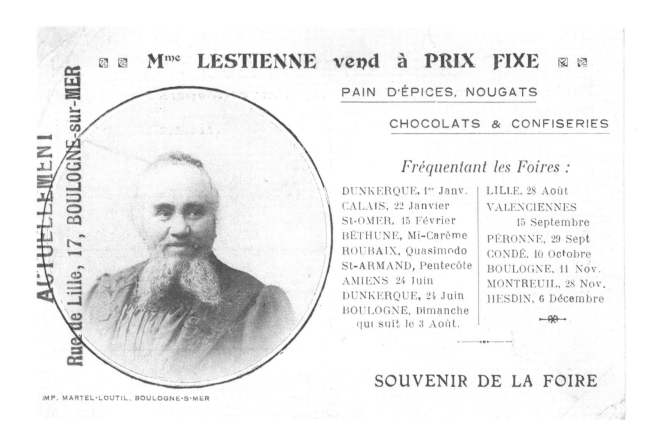

This was a concert party

La vision des combats fortifie ma vaillance;
Je vous vengerai tous... En avant, pour la France!

498

FURIA

Bonne Fête

3398

La Vie heureuse

IV.

Aux filles de bonnes maisons
Comme il avait su plaire,
Ses sujets avaient cent raisons
De le nommer leur père,
D'ailleurs il ne levait de ban
Que pour tirer quatre fois l'an
Au blanc!

HEUREUX PÈRE

L'Heure favorable.

OFFICIAL PHOTOGRAPH SHOWING BRITISH ADVANCE IN THE WEST. TAKEN BY PERMISSION OF THE C.-IN-C. OF THE B.E.F.

Supplied by The Sport & General Press Agency, Ltd., 45, Essex Street, Strand, London. **CAPTURED GERMAN TRENCHES.** Road to Loos. Crown copyright reserved. F 17868

VOILÀ DES HOMMES

Sent July 1918

Aerial photograph of the hospitals at Wimereux

On the left in the bend of the road to the sea front is the 14 General Hospital, with the sun shining on the casino roof. To the right facing the sea front is No 8 Stationary Hospital.

On the other side of the road on the right is the Australian Hospital; and on the left is the 14 Stationary Hospital. On the corner of the road is an Army Pay Corps sleeping hut and a long YMCA hut.

Proof

Made in the USA
Charleston, SC
19 June 2015

The CLASS 52s

A TRIBUTE TO THE WESTERNS

The
CLASS 52s

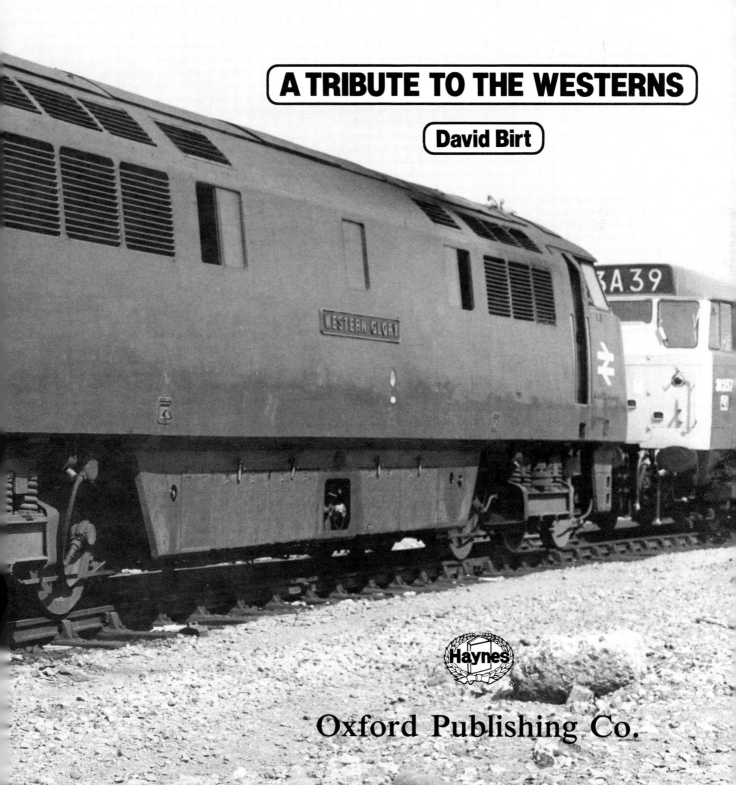

A TRIBUTE TO THE WESTERNS

David Birt

Haynes

Oxford Publishing Co.

Dedication

This book is dedicated to the men who designed and built the Class 52 Westerns. Also to all who worked on them, and to the private preservationists who preserved several of them, including:

> Mr. R. Holdsworth, Mr. D. H. Edleston, Mr. D. Rigby, Mr. K. Chinnock, The Western Locomotive Association, The Diesel Traction Group, The National Railway Museum, Foster Yeoman Ltd and the D. & E. G.

Finally to my mother Florence, without whose continued support this work would not have been made possible.

A FOULIS-OPC Railway Book

© 1988 David Birt & Haynes Publishing Group

British Library Cataloguing in Publication Data

Birt, David
    The class 52 westerns.
    1.   Great Britain. Railway services.
    British Rail. Class 52 diesel-hydraulic locomotives
    I. Title
    625.2'662'0941
    ISBN 0-86093-424-1

Published by:
Haynes Publishing Group
Sparkford, Near Yeovil, Somerset. BA22 7JJ

Haynes Publications Inc.
861 Lawrence Drive, Newbury Park, California 91320, USA

Previous page
D1072 Western Glory *makes beautiful sight at London's O. Oak Common, 25th July 1976.*

Contents

Introduction

At a meeting held at Swindon on 16th November, 1959 it was agreed to build a total of 74 locomotives. British Rail came to know them as the D1000 Class. The railway enthusiasts nicknamed them the "Wezzies". They were to succeed British Rail's Type 4, B-B, 2,200 hp Class 42, 'Warship' series hydraulics.

The work was distributed between BREL Swindon and BREL Crewe works. Initially it was planned to build two locomotive sets per month between November 1960 and January 1961 – total six sets; three locomotive sets per month between February 1961 and May 1961 – total twelve sets and four locomotive sets per month between June 1961 and July 1962 (fourteen months inclusive) making a grand total of 74 sets.

Quotations were obtained from Bristol Siddeley Engines to supply the Maybach engines, North British Locomotive Co. to supply Voith transmissions, Brush Electrical Engineering Co. Ltd. to supply control equipment and dynostarter, and finally, for Messrs. J. Stone & Co. to supply final drives, intermediate gearboxes and cardan shafts. Other equipment was put out to tender and ordered by Swindon for the full quantity of 74 locomotives.

A personal tribute to the Class 52s was first conceived during August 1976 when there were only 24 still left in running service with British Rail. At that time it was a rare occasion to see these wonderful locomotives working passenger trains in their beautiful natural surroundings of Devon and Cornwall and the photographer was wise to photograph them whenever the opportunity arose. Their appearance diminished rapidly, until by January 1977, there were only seven remaining in traffic. It was this period from Summer 1976 until February 1977 that these magnificent machines became charismatic to their following, but as their days finally closed the atmosphere became mournful, like the passing of a friend rather than that of a machine. This work I hope reflects the memories of that exciting era.

Such inscriptions as "Brave Gladiator", "I died in vain", "Thanks for the Memories", "Westerns Live On", and "Farewell My Friend", were just some of the inscriptions noted on various members of the class in their graveyard at Swindon. These feelings reflected by the enthusiast adorned the locomotives until the breaker's torch and their finality. "You served us well" was an inscription on 1025. Indeed the Westerns did serve us well. From the time of entering revenue-earning service in 1962 until the time of the last withdrawal in 1977, they covered a total of 88 million miles between them.

To the photographer, Westerns were very photogenic. They had a style of character of their own. Their lines were aesthetically pleasing, together with the distinctive sound of their Maybach engines.

Little is left to say of the Westerns which hasn't been written somewhere before. It is perhaps only one's personal feelings and experiences left open to reflect. As previously stated, the locomotives heralded a charisma and in latter days, their fanatical following was that of inspired men to great leaders. What other locomotive including any steam predecessor can claim such a following? Photographers clicked their cameras relentlessly from dawn till dusk and throughout the nights to capture the final moments. Enthusiasts would travel mile after mile just to be behind one. Direction did not matter so long as a "Wezzie" was at the head! This attraction was maintained throughout the summer of 1976 until their final demise.

The Westerns, for me, instil memories that melodies and places do for others. Their looks, their sound, their smell – there was nothing else like them – they were the flagships of the Western Region.

On 12th February 1977, whilst travelling from Derby to Birmingham by rail, I noticed numerous photographers alongside the track and at various other vantage points. It appeared to me as though a royal tour was in the offing. However, having arrived at Birmingham New Street Station, I was reminded that the British Rail "Western Finale Railtour" was due. Due to pressures on me at that time, I had not realized the eminence of this prestigious final. Luckily for me the Special was late arriving, owing to a collision with some cows just north of Yate.

First Crewe – built Western No.D1035 Western Yeoman *as turned out in July 1962 (British Railways).*

Fortunately the train managed to get moving again, but was considerably delayed. By this time the atmosphere had become tense, with everyone jostling for position to get the best possible vantage point. The train was scheduled for arrival into a crowded Platform 8. Weather conditions were poor, with a low-lying mist. I stood at the north end of the platform among many other enthusiasts in the hope of catching a first glimpse of the Special.

No one seemed sure at this stage which locomotive was heading the tour, owing to the fate described earlier. However, it was expected to be either 1013 *Western Ranger* or 1023 *Western Fusilier,* as these were the two most frequently used locomotives on specials at that time. Suddenly a voice cried ''It's 1023 *Fusilier!''.* She was easily recognised by her unique marker light panel as the tour emerged from the tunnel and through the mist into Birmingham New Street Station. She rolled in slowly, almost silent with the grace of a ship passing by. It was a very moving experience, folks applauded and cheered. Crazy! Who could understand what we saw in them? Adorning the front of the locomotive was the organiser's official plaque ''Western Finale'' symbolized by the BR official Lion and Wheel crest.

Strangely I felt proud in a way only a Western enthusiast could understand. Having paused at Birmingham for approximately ten minutes, her Maybach engines began to roar. 1023 had started to leave. I noticed the crew and the honoured look on their faces. It was a proud moment for all as the train embarked on its next leg to Derby. Once again the crowd applauded, cheered and waved. It was a very emotional

moment. Maybe I am a sentimentalist, but no other period in my lifetime including that of steam has instilled such memories for me.

Whilst on holiday in Plymouth during 1976 I contemplated this work. It was during this time I happened to see 1021 immediately after having her name and number plates removed. One of Laira's mechanics remarked, "Made a good job of painting the number on, don't you think? I'm becoming an expert at it now!" The locomotive was the victim of a shunting accident at her base depot and this was the result. I found it a particularly sad occasion to see this as I had once ridden the footplate of the locomotive from Birmingham New Street to Banbury at the kind invitation of her driver some months previously, and so it heralded special memories for me.

Yes, "'Thanks for the Memories" these wonderful locomotives gave us. For me they were part of an era I shall never forget. I hope my acknowledgement of the class will do justice and give an everlasting pleasure to the ardent admirer, as I have been given many times before.

In addition to my photographic collection I have included an historical survey of the last seven Westerns remaining in service with British Rail by January 1977. Although the railtours mentioned have had previous excellent documentation by others, I feel it only fitting that as these played such a major role in the final months of the locomotives, they should be included in my text.

Since final withdrawals there have been no less than seven Westerns preserved; a fitting tribute to this ever-popular diesel class locomotive.

David Birt
1988

The fully restored D1041 Western Prince at BREL Crewe Works on 4th February 1988. It is positioned on No. 4 road in front of the traverser outside the Erecting Shop. The livery is maroon with Crewe style buffer beam and apron in yellow up to the beading and over the recessed area.

An Unforgettable Experience

One evening during the Autumn of 1975, I had decided to go for an evening out at the local dance in Birmingham. Instinct told me before proceeding to the venue to have a look in at Birmingham New Street Station first, just to see what was doing. To my sheer delight, there she was, standing at Platform 1 awaiting departure for Paddington; D1021 *Western Cavalier*.

The driver and second man, both Old Oak Common men, were taking a short break sitting adjacent to the locomotive at the side of the platform. We got talking and, of course, I just had to express my enthusiasm for their magnificent machine. "It's alright for you blokes," the driver exclaimed, "you don't have to drive the bloody things!"

"What do you mean?" was my innocent reply.

"Ever been on the cakewalk at a fair?" he said. "Well it's about the same as that at around 60, and you can't breathe either because there's no ventilation. If you open the side window a little the sound deafens you. If you open it further, the wind blows your head off."

I just could not believe his disparaging remarks about this superb looking locomotive.

"What are you doing now," he said.

"Nothing," I quickly replied.

"If you would like to come as far as Banbury with us, I will show you what I mean."

Immediately I climbed into the cab. By this time I had completely forgotten about the dance. I saw the signal light change to green and heard the guard's whistle blow. My heart missed a beat. *Cavalier* and her ten coach load started to roll under Birmingham New Street's south end tunnel. We crawled round a tight bend as the train passed Bordesley Green, but then started to gather speed on the approach to Tyseley and Acocks Green. How can you describe such a sensation as this marvellous footplate ride? Past Acocks Green and 1021 was approaching the dreaded speed, almost 60 mph was now recording on the speedometer.

"Here we go", the driver remarked. It was better than the fair ride described earlier because of the sensation of speed as well. The locomotive bounced up and down and rocked from side to side – I began to think we were going to de-rail at any time.

"Are you feeling warm," the train driver remarked, "I can't open the window otherwise you will get your ruddy head blown off. You will just have to sweat it out."

I looked at the speedometer again, which was now recording 80 to 90 mph and the ride had now levelled out to a smooth glide. It was my life's most exhilarating experience, thanks to those kind men from Old Oak Common.

I waved good-bye at Banbury. *Cavalier* growled away with two black plumes of smoke from her characteristic exhaust. The driver waved back as the train disappeared into the distance.

That was the last I saw of 1021 until my holiday in Plymouth in August 1976, where we met up again but this time in less happy circumstances. She had just had her number painted on the cab side, the death mark of all Westerns. *Cavalier* had been withdrawn due to a shunting accident and was now about to join the line up for scrap . . .

D1021 Western Cavalier *at Laira,*
15th August 1976.

The Class 52 Westerns

D1000	WESTERN ENTERPRISE	D1037	WESTERN EMPRESS
D1001	WESTERN PATHFINDER	D1038	WESTERN SOVEREIGN
D1002	WESTERN EXPLORER	D1039	WESTERN KING
D1003	WESTERN PIONEER	D1040	WESTERN QUEEN
D1004	WESTERN CRUSADER	D1041	WESTERN PRINCE
D1005	WESTERN VENTURER	D1042	WESTERN PRINCESS
D1006	WESTERN STALWART	D1043	WESTERN DUKE
D1007	WESTERN TALISMAN	D1044	WESTERN DUCHESS
D1008	WESTERN HARRIER	D1045	WESTERN VISCOUNT
D1009	WESTERN INVADER	D1046	WESTERN MARQUIS
D1010	WESTERN CAMPAIGNER	D1047	WESTERN LORD
D1011	WESTERN THUNDERER	D1048	WESTERN LADY
D1012	WESTERN FIREBRAND	D1049	WESTERN MONARCH
D1013	WESTERN RANGER	D1050	WESTERN RULER
D1014	WESTERN LEVIATHAN	D1051	WESTERN AMBASSADOR
D1015	WESTERN CHAMPION	D1052	WESTERN VICEROY
D1016	WESTERN GLADIATOR	D1053	WESTERN PATRIARCH
D1017	WESTERN WARRIOR	D1054	WESTERN GOVERNOR
D1018	WESTERN BUCCANEER	D1055	WESTERN ADVOCATE
D1019	WESTERN CHALLENGER	D1056	WESTERN SULTAN
D1020	WESTERN HERO	D1057	WESTERN CHIEFTAIN
D1021	WESTERN CAVALIER	D1058	WESTERN NOBLEMAN
D1022	WESTERN SENTINEL	D1059	WESTERN EMPIRE
D1023	WESTERN FUSILIER	D1060	WESTERN DOMINION
D1024	WESTERN HUNTSMAN	D1061	WESTERN ENVOY
D1025	WESTERN GUARDSMAN	D1062	WESTERN COURIER
D1026	WESTERN CENTURION	D1063	WESTERN MONITOR
D1027	WESTERN LANCER	D1064	WESTERN REGENT
D1028	WESTERN HUSSAR	D1065	WESTERN CONSORT
D1029	WESTERN LEGIONNAIRE*	D1066	WESTERN PREFECT
D1030	WESTERN MUSKETEER	D1067	WESTERN DRUID
D1031	WESTERN RIFLEMAN	D1068	WESTERN RELIANCE
D1032	WESTERN MARKSMAN	D1069	WESTERN VANGUARD
D1033	WESTERN TROOPER	D1070	WESTERN GAUNTLET
D1034	WESTERN DRAGOON	D1071	WESTERN RENOWN
D1035	WESTERN YEOMAN	D1072	WESTERN GLORY
D1036	WESTERN EMPEROR	D1073	WESTERN BULWARK

*Named WESTERN LEGIONAIRE until 1967.

Official British Railways view of D1035 Western Yeoman.
(British Rail)

Western Genesis

The 'Warship' class diesel hydraulics were the Class 52's predecessors. As a development of Germany's K-M V200 locomotive, they entered service with British Rail Western Region during August 1958.

They were the first British built locomotives to employ a stressed skin structure, a method of construction more commonly used in the aviation and structural steel industries. This gives an excellent strength-to-weight ratio which would be needed for a 2,000 bhp locomotive on four axles and under 80 tons all-on weight. With this method there was no separate underframe and the locomotive sides and roof became stress bearers which contributed to the overall strength of the structure.

During construction, body side panels would be offered up to a lattice of folded steel angle Z and other sections. Panels would then be tack welded to the framework and later stressed by heating with oxy-acetylene equipment, then cooled rapidly with water, thus shrinking the metal skin and adding to the strength of the whole locomotive structure. However, with this method of manufacture it became necessary to coat the structure with an anti-corrosive substance (Prestolith) before painting. This technique of manufacture was later used for the Class 52 Westerns, H.S.T. vehicles, certain diesel electric locomotives and modern rolling stock.

It was in 1959 that the Western Region envisaged greater brake horsepower would be required than that supplied by their new 'Warship' diesels in order to work heavier loads and accelerated timetables.

At this time Krauss-Maffei of Germany had developed a 3,000 hp C-C version of their V200 locomotive known as the ML3000, drawings of which were sent by K-M to the W.R., in accordance with a promise given to the Swindon's chief draughtsman during a visit to Munich. However, owing to the restrictions of the British loading gauge the mechanical layout of the ML3000 could not be followed to any great extent and communications regarding the locomotive with K-M gradually ceased.

Minimum of change had previously been made in the design of the D800 'Warship' from Germany's V200. However, in the case of the D1000 Class the B.T.C. Chief Mechanical Engineer was known to have had a free hand. Hence, the stated responsibility of Smeddle and Swindon Works, was a detailed design and construction of the locomotive. As a result of the above-mentioned developments, between 1961 and 1964, perhaps the most handsome diesels in the World emerged from Swindon and Crewe Works respectively.

D1056 Western Sultan *posed outside Old Oak Common Depot, 8th August 1976.*

D1034 Western Dragoon awaits departure on a West of England train at Paddington, c1970.

'Warship' series D800 Class No. 818 Glory, seen here in Swindon yard on the 7th November 1976 as a static exhibit. This locomotive was built at these works on the 30.3.60 and was withdrawn on the 1.11.72. They were the forerunners of the D1000 'Westerns'.

A cut-away view of the Bristol
Siddeley Maybach MD 655 12
cylinder engine as used in the
Westerns.
(Courtesy Russell Carter)

Early Days

Left: No. D1000 *Western Enterprise*, in desert sand livery, arrives at Birmingham Snow Hill on 30th August 1962 at the head of the 06.30 Birkenhead–Paddington train.

(M. Mensing)

Right: No. D1002 *Western Explorer*, in green livery, on exhibition at Birmingham Snow Hill on 10th April 1962 during "Western Rail Week".

(M. Mensing)

Below: No. D1003 *Western Pioneer* approaches Acocks Green station with the 12.10 Paddington–Birkenhead working on 4th June 1963.

(M. Mensing)

Westerns in Action

Above: No. D1065 *Western Consort* leaves Harbury Tunnel, near Leamington Spa with the 15.10 Paddington–Wolverhampton (Low Level) on 17th August 1963.

(M. Mensing)

Below: No. D1008 *Western Harrier* heads the 'up' ''Cambrian Coast Express'' past Acocks Green, Birmingham on 17th September 1962.

(M. Mensing)

Above: No. D1023 *Western Fusilier* of the National Collection is seen at Goodrington Sands station on the Torbay & Dartmouth Railway, 5th September 1981.

(*S.N. Crowther*)

Above: No. D1048 *Western Lady* at Grosmont, North Yorkshire Moors Railway, 28th April 1979. Although restored in green livery this is non authentic for this locomotive. Delivered new in maroon livery, it was the first of the class to receive rail blue livery with all-yellow ends. It was later moved to Steamport, Southport.

(*P.D. Nicholson*)

Left: No. D1062 *Western Courier*, pride of the Western Locomotive Association and kept on the Severn Valley Railway. A close up view of the 'B' end, photographed on a visit to the Birmingham Railway Museum, Tyseley, 2nd October 1987.

Western Details

(All No. D1041 *Western Prince*, Crewe, 4th February 1988.)

Above left: A roof top view looking towards the 'B' (coach emblem) end.

Above: Cab window detail showing the brass restoration plaque, number plate and route disc on the 'A' end.

Left: Cab interior with control desk, driver's seat and handbrake wheel.

Below left: Buffer beam and headcode indicator panel.

Below right: Bogie details including speedometer.

Western Design

The Westerns were basically a C-C version (6 axle) of the D800 'Warship' series hydraulics, employing the same basic principles of bogie and superstructure design. Body styling was the result of collaboration between Swindon's drawing office and Professor Misha Black's Design Research Unit.

At a meeting held at Swindon drawing office on the 26th November 1958 a suggestion was passed by Christian Barman, author of the GWR's *Next Station,* to Mr. K. W. C. Grand, General Manager of the Western Region, 'That the 2,700 hp locomotive should be designed with a distinctive styling which would be recognised as typically Western Region''. It is without doubt that they must have been well pleased, for out of this concept emerged one of the most handsome diesels in Europe if not the World.

The power units installed in the Western were basically the same as the Maybach MD650 version as installed in their 'Warship' predecessors. However, the MD655 version installed in the Westerns had the addition of charge-air cooling in order to give the required increased power output (ie 1,350 hp @ 1,500 rpm ea x 2 = 2,700 hp total). Westerns also employed the most modern version of the Voith three-converter transmission system (Model L630 r U) of the L306 r pattern previously installed in 33 of the D800 'Warship' class.

Initially the Westerns had poor riding qualities and were subjected to numerous failures due to transmission defects. However the latter was not the fault of the Voith transmission or the Maybach–designed axle drive but in poor bogie design. Unknown at that time the transmission defects were being oscillated through the cardan shafts from the bogies. Apparently, the fault lay with the torque reaction arms employed in the Krauss-Maffei design. These were the cause of torsional vibrations being set up in the output shaft bearing cages due to their insufficient resilience to cope with shocks from the track and changes from drive to coast. This inevitably caused early bearing seizures and transmission failures.

The poor riding qualities experienced with the D1000 class were due to the link and bell crank system of design employed to give a virtual centre. This concept was subjected to misgivings by BR in its inability to permit freedom of movement laterally of a traditional bogie design. These turned out to be justifiable when track irregularities produced severe lateral body accelerations. Rectification of the problem was simply to remove the Krauss-Maffei link and crank motion, leaving the control of lateral and rotational movement to the swing links, an arrangement similar to the Dean bogie of the GWR.

By the time a new revised bogie design evolved from Swindon, locomotives D1030 to D1034, now transferred from Swindon to Crewe and the last of the batch to be built, were the only members of the class to receive the modified design from new.

Cab ventilation in the majority of the Western fleet proved inadequate from the driver's point of view. The only method of obtaining fresh air or ventilation was through the cab sliding window which only proved to be noisy and uncomfortable for him. However, locomotives, D1012, D1028, D1039, D1056 and D1071 were all fitted with a cab ventilation system distinguished by a small square panel at the front of the locomotive, situated just below the windscreen to the left hand side off centre. D1045 and D1052 had a similar arrangement fitted in the roof indicated by two small square panels mounted either side of the central window panel under the roof lip.

Other external variations which applied to the class during their working life were those of experimental windscreen wipers. Locomotives D1006 and D1039 were tested with a nautical rotary type for a while which was driven by a small electric motor. D1045 was unique in having one wiper mounted to the top of the windscreen driver's side, and one to the bottom second man's side. Finally, locomotives D1020, D1023, D1053 and D1055 all had experimental side action type wipers fitted to the driver's side only.

The only other external detail deviation known to the author was the removal of train headboard brackets from various members of the class.

D1000 Western Enterprise *in ex works condition at Swindon. Note the 'D' has been painted over on the numberplate. (R. C. H. Nash).*

D1001 Western Pathfinder. *An unusual shot of this locomotive at its base depot, Laira 15th August 1976. The distinctive external springing and speedometer cable can be seen clearly in this picture*

1001 at rest in Exeter sidings,
3th August 1976.

ogie detail of the preserved
1041 Western Prince.

Front end close-up of D1041 a[s]
restored at Crewe in 1988.

Details of D1041 as it is today: The
front apron.

Lower door details showing foothole and kick plate.

Close-up of the Smiths speedometer.

Cab interior of Western Prince, February 1988.

The Crewe Connection

Three main reasons have been quoted offically as to why 44 locomotives were built at Crewe.
1. To give an even workload between the two works.
2. Crewe had a better reputation for delivery dates.
3. Costs at Crewe were traditionally lower than Swindon. Eg the Crewe built 9F class 2-10-0s had been 15% cheaper than the Swindon built examples.

The initial order for 39 locomotives from Crewe, Order No. E507, Account Lot 286 was at a unit cost of £115,500. A further order for ten locomotives was later reduced to five, these being Lot 286 also.

The Voith transmissions were made by Heidenham who supplied 60 sets and North British Locomotive Co. and subsequently Voith Engineering (Glasgow) Ltd following liquidation of NBL. The two latter companies supplied 103 transmission sets making a total of 163, being two for each locomotive plus 15 spare sets.

Both Swindon and Crewe experienced production problems with locomotives in a semi-complete state due to delays in receiving the transmission sets. This was the prime cause of production being out of numerical sequence and the sanctioned price being exceeded by a few thousand pounds, but Crewe was still the cheaper of the two. The second order to Crewe came about because of the production delays at Swindon and the urgent need for the locomotives, due to the accelerated dieselisation programme on the Western Region. A further suggested reason for the use of Crewe was that it would give another workshop on BR experience with hydraulic transmissions in addition to Swindon.

The last two Westerns under construction at Crewe in 1963 – D103 Western Trooper and D103 Western Dragoon.

(Keith Collier

D1030 Western Musketeer outside the Crewe Paint Shop when brand new, December 1963.

(Keith Collier

Technical Specification

Nos   D1000 – D1073
Class (TOPS)   52
Builder   British Railways, Swindon and Crewe Works
Date built   1961 – 1964
Parent Office   Swindon
Operational Region   Western

Overall Dimensions:
Length over Buffers   68 ft
Max. Height   13 ft 1 in
Max. Width   9 ft

Distance Between:
Bogie Centres   42 ft 6 in
Bogie Wheel Base   12 ft 2 in
Wheel Dia.   3 ft 7 in
Journal Size   190 mm x 243 mm

Bearings:
Maker   Skefco
Type   Roller

Wheel Arrangement   C-C
Min. Radius Curve   4$\frac{1}{2}$ chains

Max. Speed   90 mph

Tractive Effort:
Starting   66,770 lbs
  67,388 lbs Dual Braked
Continuous   45,200 Dual Braked
  @ 14.5 mph

Locomotive Weight:
Empty   98.4 Tons
  101.3 Tons Dual Brake
Full   108 Tons
  109 Tons Dual Braked

Distribution

*	*	*	*	*	*
18.25	18.25	17.75	17.8	18.0	17.95

Dual Braked:

*	*	*	*	*	*
18.35	18.4	17.6	18.5	18.0	18.15

Ratio H.P.   2 760
HP/WT Ratio   25.36
  25.32 Dual Braked

Engine:
No. of units   Two
Maker   Maybach
Type   MD 655
Bore   195 mm
Stroke   200 mm
Max. speed   1500 rpm

Fuel Injection Equipment:
Combined Fuel Injector   L'Orange IV
Fuel Oil Total   850 Galls
Lub Oil Total each   50 Galls
Cooling Water Total each   175 Galls

Transmission:
Maker   Voith
Type   L6-30rV
Oil Total each   95 Galls

Intermediate Gearbox:
Maker   Stone Maybach
Type   B76
  W430
Oil Total each   3$\frac{1}{4}$ Galls

Final drive
Maker   Stone Maybach
Type   C33VC
Oil Total each   2$\frac{1}{2}$ Galls

Cardan Shafts:
Engine to Transmission
Maker   Stone

Other Drives:
Transmission: Dynostarter Hardy Spicer
  Serck Fan Pump Hardy Spicer

Heat Exchanger:
Engine Maker   Serck
Transmission Maker   Serck
Radiator Elements, No.   96
Maker   Serck
Air Filters, No   8
Maker   Vokes

Train Heating Boiler:
Maker   Spanner Mark A
Evap. Capacity   2000 lbs/hr
Fuel Oil   See Main Tank
Feed Water   980 Galls
  800 Dual Braked

Type of Brake:
  Laycock
  Knorr
  West/n
  Laycock Dual Braked
  Knorr

Vacuum Exhauster:
No.   Two
Maker   Westinghouse
Delivery Capacity each   110 ft^3 @ 1000 rpm

Compressor:
No.   One
No.   Two Dual Braked
Maker   Laycock
  Knorr
  Laycock Knorr Dual Braked
  Westinghouse
Type   W100
  100 GB
  DO
  3 VC 50 Dual Braked
Delivery Capacity each   28 ft^3
  1000 rpm
  DO 50 of Westinghouse
  1050 rpm Dual Braked

Electricity Equipment:
Batteries
Maker   Crompton Parkinson
Type   HA 25
Capacity   280 Amps Hr
No. Cells   48

Dynostarter or Generator:
Maker   Brush
Type   TG 42-36
Control Equipment
Maker   Brush

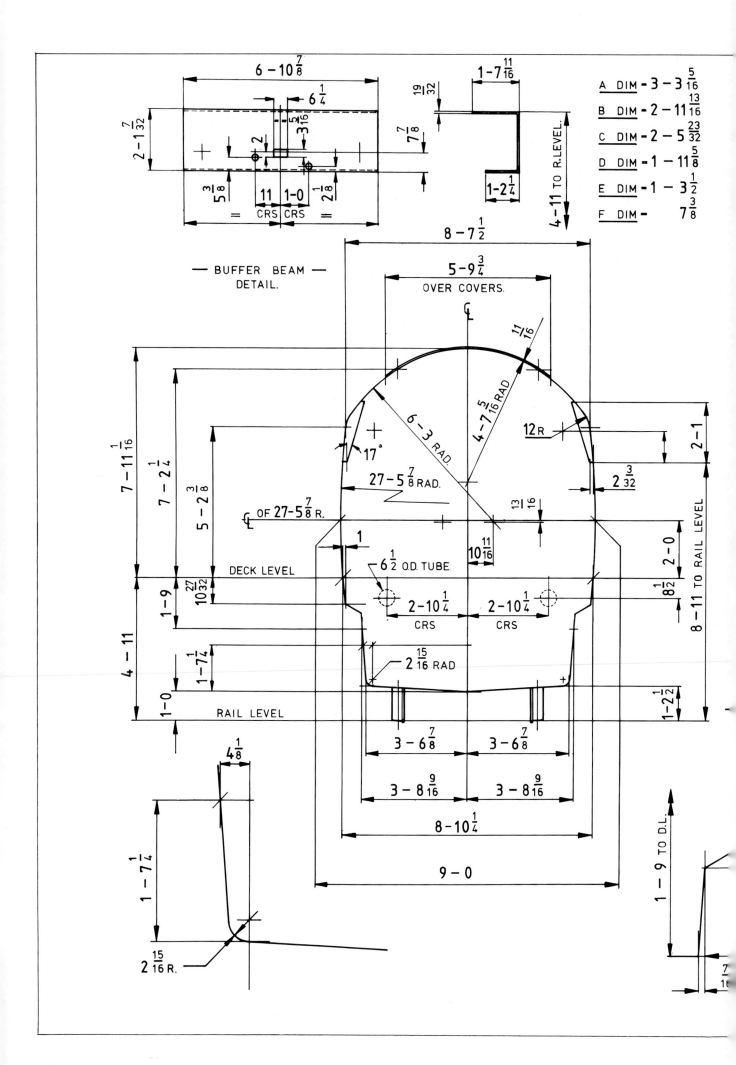

— BUFFER BEAM —
DETAIL.

A DIM - 3 - 3 $\frac{5}{16}$
B DIM - 2 - 11 $\frac{13}{16}$
C DIM - 2 - 5 $\frac{23}{32}$
D DIM - 1 - 11 $\frac{5}{8}$
E DIM - 1 - 3 $\frac{1}{2}$
F DIM - 7 $\frac{3}{8}$

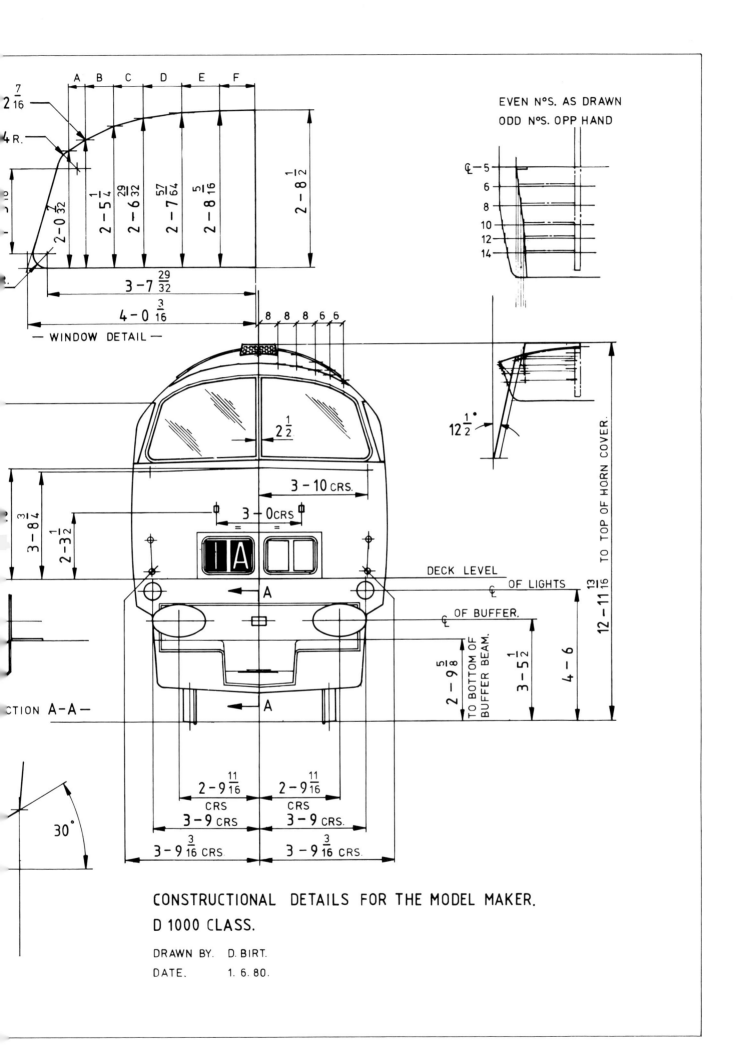

— WINDOW DETAIL —

SECTION A-A —

CONSTRUCTIONAL DETAILS FOR THE MODEL MAKER.

D 1000 CLASS.

DRAWN BY. D. BIRT.

DATE. 1. 6. 80.

Underframe Construction

The underframe portion was built up round the two substantial tubular members running from buffer beam to buffer beam. Assemblies of longitudinal and transverse plates were welded up, slid along the outside of the tubes, and then the whole welded up as one. These plate assemblies included deep centre vertical-plate sections in which the fuel tanks were suspended; the boiler water tank itself being immediately below the boiler, on the top deck plate which covered more or less the full length and breadth of the locomotive.

1.   SIDE PLATE (LONG)
2.   SIDE PLATE (SHORT)
3.   INNER STRETCHER
4.   END STRETCHER
9.   OUTER STRETCHER
11.   FLANGE STRIP
14.   RIB
18.   RIB
19.   RIB

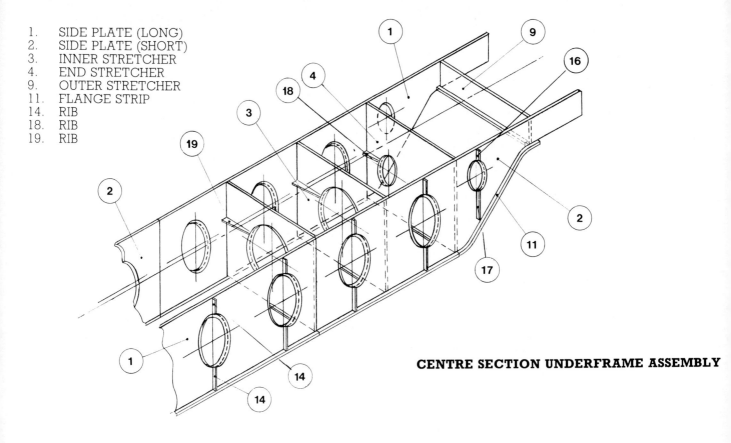

CENTRE SECTION UNDERFRAME ASSEMBLY

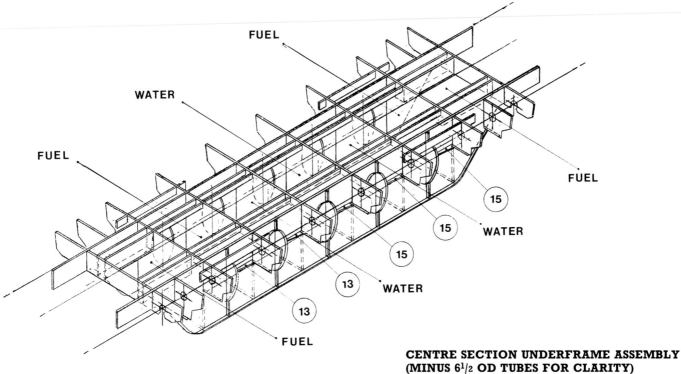

**CENTRE SECTION UNDERFRAME ASSEMBLY
(MINUS 6¹/₂ OD TUBES FOR CLARITY)
SHOWING FUEL AND WATER TANK POSITION.**

CENTRE SECTION UNDERFRAME
PARTS LIST IDENTIFICATION

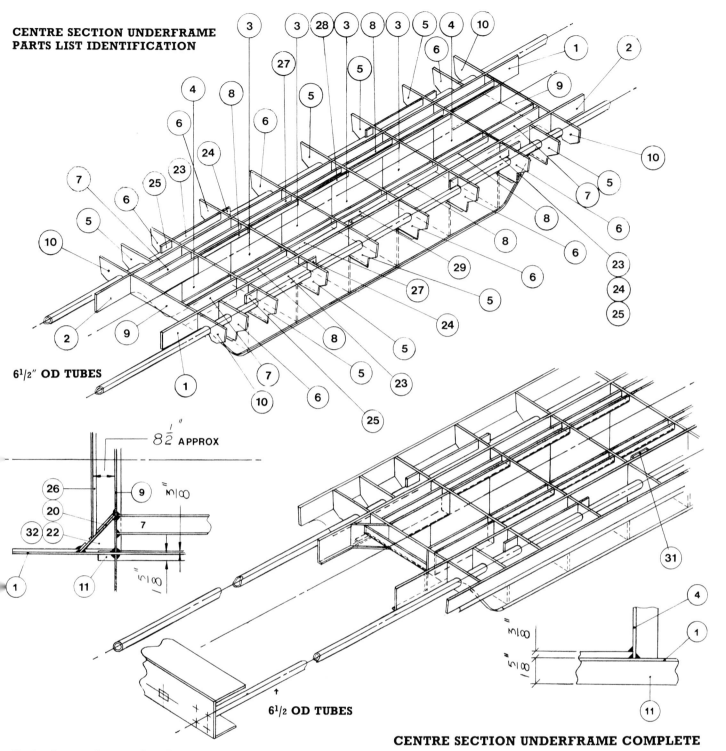

6¹/₂" OD TUBES

8½" APPROX

6¹/₂ OD TUBES

Underframe Centre Section

CENTRE SECTION UNDERFRAME COMPLETE

Item				Item		
1	SIDE PLATE (LONG)	– 2 OFF		18	RIB	– 4 OFF
2	SIDE PLATE (SHORT)	– 2 OFF		19	RIB	– 8 OFF
3	INNER STRETCHER	– 4 OFF		20	ANGLE PLATE	– 4 OFF
4	END STRETCHER	– 2 OFF		21		
5	WING PLATE	– 8 OFF		22	FILL IN PLATE	– 2 OFF
6	WING PLATE	– 8 OFF		23	RIB PLATE	– 4 OFF
7	TANK CARRIER	– 4 OFF		24	RIB PLATE	– 4 OFF
8	TANK CARRIER	– 6 OFF		25	RIB PLATE	– 4 OFF
9	OUTER STRETCHER	– 2 OFF		26	STIFFENING PLATE	– 2 OFF
10	OUTER WING PLATE	– 4 OFF		27	TANK CARRIER	– 2 OFF
11	FLANGE STRIP	– 4 OFF		28	TANK CARRIER	– 1 OFF
12	PAD (T.C.)	– 56 OFF		29	TANK CARRIER	– 1 OFF
13	RIB	– 8 OFF		30	TUBE (T.C.)	– 2 OFF
14	RIB	– 20 OFF		31	SUPPORT	– 1 OFF
15	RIB	– 12 OFF		32	FILL IN PLATE (OPPOSITE HAND)	– 2 OFF
16	RIB	– 4 OFF				
17	RIB	– 4 OFF		(T.C.) – Tank Carrier Component		

Hydraulic Transmission

The main attraction of the hydraulic transmission system over that of its electric counterpart, is its light weight. This feature was recognised by the Western Region and it was envisaged that a hydraulic locomotive weighing less than 80 tons would give a greater power output than an electric locomotive of 2,000 hp weighing more than 130 tons.

First, to consider a diesel engine as a single unit, this may be very efficient. However, its characteristics do not make it suitable for a direct drive from the crankshaft to the driving axle. In order to obtain an effective torque at the axle, the high-speed low-torque characteristics of the diesel engine must be converted via means of an intermediate transmission system. This cannot take a purely mechanical form owing to the heavy loads incurred when starting a train in the higher power ranges. The alternative is either to use a diesel engine to generate electricity, which drives the wheels via means of an electric traction motor; or to employ a special form of flexible transmission. This latter system (as with electric) must be capable of affording infinitely variable conversion and effective control over the whole range of power output, if full advantage is to be made of the diesel engine. A locomotive employing this form of system is known as diesel-hydraulic. The transmission system consists of an oil filled torque converter, interposed between the crankshaft of the diesel engine and gearbox (if fitted). (See Fig. 1.) Alternatively, two or more convertors can be used instead of a gearbox. The former would comprise of three basic parts:

i)   The centrifugal pump, or impeller (which would be driven by the engine).
ii) The turbine or output member fixed to the output shaft (which would drive the wheels through the appropriate gearing).
iii) Finally, the fixed guide wheel or stator.

(All being mounted co-axially and contained in an oil-filled casing.)

In operation, the input (or engine) shaft turns the impeller, whose blades force the oil (by centrifugal force) onto the blades of the turbine, (fixed to the output shaft), thus imparting a torque which makes it rotate. The oil then passes to the vanes of the fixed guide wheel which divert it back to the impeller blades. This action reciprocates the oil to be continually circulated whilst the torque converter is in use. The converter is so designed that the torque transmission to the turbine rises as the turbine speed drops, thus making it ideally suitable for the well known locomotive requirements. Hence, the lower the locomotive speed, the greater is the pulling power. This characteristic also provides a smooth, shock-free drive between the engine and locomotive wheels over the whole range of engine power.

One of the 60 L630rV hydraulic transmission units delivered in 1961 by Voith of Heidenheim, West Germany to the North British Locomotive Co., Glasgow for the D1000 class locomotives.
(Courtesy Russell Carter)

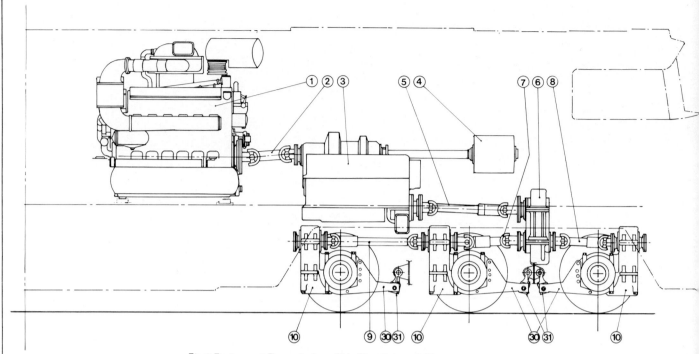

Fig.1. Engine and Transmission Side Elevation and Plan.

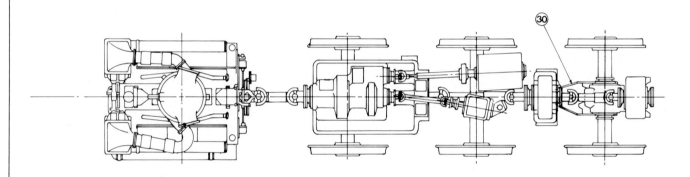

W R, CLASS 52, TRANSMISSION LAYOUT.

© R.S. Carter

1. Maybach Engine MD 655 12 cyl: 1380 HP at 1500 RPM
2. Cardan Shaft; engine to transmission Type 267/6
3. Voith transmission block Type L 630V
4. Dynostarter
5. Cardan shaft Type 267/7. Transmission to Inter: gearbox
6. Stone-Maybach Inter: gearbox B76W.430
7. Cardan shaft 267/6 model L.1
8. Cardan shaft 167/5^1/2 52 model L.2
9. Cardan shaft 167/5^1/2 52 std model.
10. Stone Maybach final drive C.33.V.
11. Bogie Frame
12. Guide Linkage
13. Main Body frame, downward protruding.
14. Hard manganese liners
15. Axlebox thrust faces
16. Bogie transoms

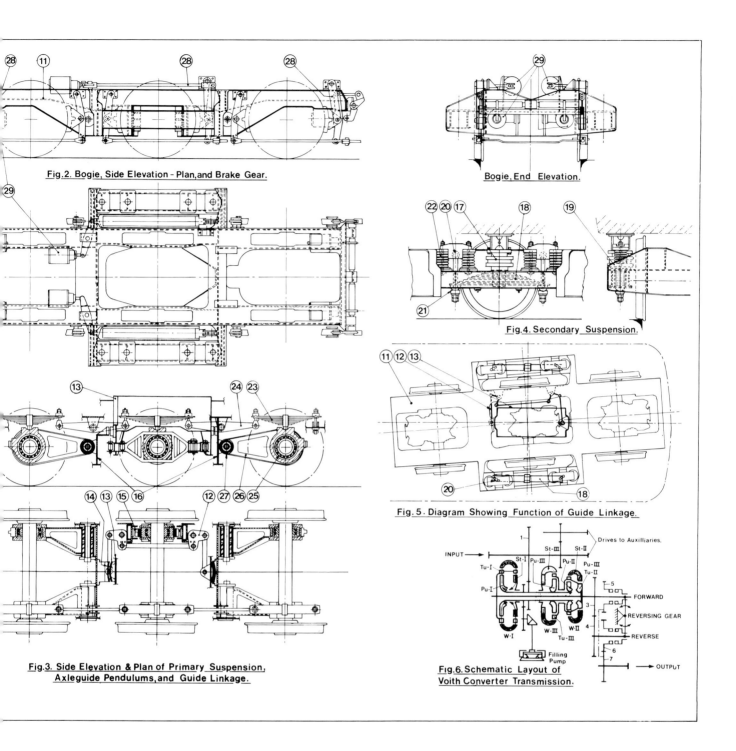

Fig.2. Bogie, Side Elevation - Plan,and Brake Gear.

Bogie, End Elevation.

Fig.4. Secondary Suspension.

Fig.3. Side Elevation & Plan of Primary Suspension,
Axleguide Pendulums,and Guide Linkage.

Fig.5. Diagram Showing Function of Guide Linkage.

Fig.6. Schematic Layout of
Voith Converter Transmission.

17. Rubber bolster support
18. Underframe laminated spring for secondary springing.
19. Cantilevered frame.
20. Spring hangers.
21. Rocking washers.
22. Helical spring for secondary springing.
23. Laminated axle spring for primary springing.
24. Equalising beams
25. SKF taper roller bearing axle box.
26. Pendulum axle guides.
27. Silentbloc type bushings.
28. Brake rigging
29. Pneumatic brake operating cylinder
30. Torque Reaction arm.
31. Rubber suspension arm.

Western Withdrawals

Withdrawal of the Westerns commenced on the 6th May 1973. First to go were D1032 *Western Marksman* together with D1019 *Western Challenger*, the former having completed only 944,000 miles at the time of withdrawal, which was the lowest recorded mileage of the Western fleet. Further withdrawals took place on 4th June 1973 when D1018 *Western Buccaneer* and D1020 *Western Hero* were condemned. These were shortly followed on the 21st July 1973 by D1039 *Western King* and D1042 *Western Princess*. On the 1st August 1973 D1004 *Western Crusader* and D1017 *Western Warrior* were also condemned.

Locomotives D1017, D1018, D1019 and D1020 were the only members of the class not to have been fitted with the D.A.W.S. and dual braking systems at this period in time.

The final withdrawals which took place in that year were on the 8th October, when D1038 *Western Sovereign* was withdrawn, followed on the 18th November by D1024 *Western Huntsman* and D1060 *Western Dominion*, this making a grand total of eleven Western withdrawals for the year 1973.

The following year saw the same amount of ·Class 52s disappear from the railway scene, until by the end of 1975 only 34 remained in active service.

Many of the Western condemnations were due to British Rail's programme of planned withdrawal. This was a system of cannibalisation employed to keep the remaining fleet running as long as possible with an adequate supply of spares.

It can be seen clearly from the accompanying table, that during the latter years the class seemed very prone to mishaps. From 1974 onwards, members were withdrawn through either collisions or derailment damage. D1000 *Western Enterprise* and D1001 *Western Pathfinder*, both "possibles" for preservation, were only finally condemned to the scrap yard because of this fate.

D1021 Western Cavalier, *Laira, 15th August 1976 – showing the "cause of death"* . . .

Locomotive	Built*	Withdrawn	Reason	Disposal†	Final Mileage (x 1,000)
1000 Enterprise	29.12.61	11.2.74	'A' end collision damage	Swindon 14.3.74	1,240
1001 Pathfinder	12.2.62	4.10.76	'B' end collision damage	Swindon 4.1.77	1,264
1002 Explorer	19.3.62	29.1.74	'B' end collision damage	Swindon 29.1.74	1,144
1003 Pioneer	14.4.62	5.1.75	Waiting engines	Swindon 28.5.75	1,248
1004 Crusader	12.5.62	1.8.73	Planned withdrawal	Swindon 1.8.73	1,088
1005 Venturer	18.6.62	16.11.76	'A' end Dynostarter and cables burnt	Swindon 5.1.77	1,392
1006 Stalwart	6.7.62	6.4.75	Waiting engines	Swindon 8.9.75	1,208
1007 Talisman	1.8.62	29.1.74	De-railed 19.12.73 West Ealing	Swindon 18.2.74	1,160
1008 Harrier	4.9.62	21.10.74	Waiting engines	Swindon 9.1.75	1,136
1009 Invader	24.9.62	10.11.76	Planned withdrawal	Engines and cooler sold to Dutch scrap dealer. Remains Swindon 1.6.77	1,376
1010 Campaigner	15.10.62	28.2.77	Planned withdrawal	Stored at N.A. 3.3.77 Sold: Foster Yeoman Co. Shepton Mallet 5/77	1,360
1011 Thunderer	27.10.62	6.10.75	Planned withdrawal	Swindon 24.11.75	1,248
1012 Firebrand	17.11.62	2.11.75	Planned withdrawal	Swindon 28.4.76	1,296
1013 Ranger	13.12.62	28.2.77	Planned withdrawal	Stored at N.A. 3.3.77 Sold: Richard Holdsworth, Reading 5/77	1,320
1014 Leviathan	24.12.62	6.8.74	Waiting bogies and engines	Swindon 30.9.74	1,128
1015 Champion	21.1.63	13.12.76	Derailment damage	Swindon 4.1.77	1,296
1016 Gladiator	16.2.63	29.12.75	'A' end Dynostart and wire fire	Swindon 12.5.76	1,248
1017 Warrior	15.3.63	1.8.73	Waiting engines	Swindon 1.8.73	984
1018 Buccaneer	2.4.63	4.6.73	Waiting engines and due 'FX'	Swindon 30.7.73	968
1019 Challenger	3.5.63	6.5.73	Waiting engines and due 'FX'	Swindon 30.7.73	968
1020 Hero	21.5.63	4.6.73	Waiting engines and due 'FX'	Swindon 13.11.73	968
1021 Cavalier	17.6.63.	10.8.76	Collision damage	Swindon 23.9.76	1,280
1022 Sentinel	16.7.63	18.1.77	Derailment damage at Old Oak Common	Swindon 11.5.77	1,312
1023 Fusilier	23.9.63	28.2.77	Planned withdrawal	N.R.M. 27.2.77	1,256
1024 Huntsman	1.10.63	18.11.73	Waiting engines and due 'FX'	Swindon 14.3.74	984
1025 Guardsman	·1.11.63.	6.10.75	Planned withdrawal	Swindon 28.4.76	1,192
1026 Centurion	24.12.63	6.10.75	Planned withdrawal	Swindon 10.11.75	1,144
1027 Lancer	28.1.64	2.11.75	Planned withdrawal	Swindon 9.2.76	1,176
1028 Hussar	25.2.64	6.10.76	Collision damage	Swindon 18.10.76	1,256
1029 Legionnaire	20.4.64	18.11.74	Collision damage 'A' end	Swindon 5.3.75	1,056
1030 Musketeer	5.12.63	19.4.76	Collision damage 'B' end	Swindon 12.5.76	1,216
1031 Rifleman	20.12.63	1.2.75	Waiting for engines and fire damage	Swindon 28.5.75	1,096
1032 Marksman	31.12.63	6.5.73	Axle flaw and 'F' exam	Swindon 29.1.74	944
1033 Trooper	17.1.64	17.9.76	'B' bogie thin tyres	Swindon 24.3.77	1,272
1034 Dragoon	15.4.64	6.10.75	Frame fracture of main tube	Swindon 23.9.76	1,144
1035 Yeoman	27.7.62	5.1.75	Waiting engines and fire damage	Swindon 28.5.75	1,176
1036 Emperor	29.8.62	1.11.76	Planned withdrawal	Swindon 22.11.76	1,360

Locomotive	Built*	Withdrawn	Reason	Disposal†	Final Mileage (x 1,000)
D1037 Empress	31.8.62	24.5.76	Derailment damage	Swindon 21.9.76	1,336
D1038 Sovereign	7.9.62	8.10.73	Underframe damage	Swindon 29.1.74	1,072
D1039 King	7.9.62	21.7.73	Waiting engines and due 'FX'	Swindon 13.11.73	1,024
D1040 Queen	20.9.62	29.2.76	Planned withdrawal	Swindon 3.5.76	1,248
D1041 Prince	10.10.62	23.2.77	'B' end Dynostart burnt out	Stored at N.A. 25.2.77 Sold David Edleston, Derby 5/77	1,384
D1042 Princess	19.10.62	21.7.73	Planned withdrawal	Swindon 29.1.74	976
D1043 Duke	26.10.62	4.4.76	Planned withdrawal	Swindon 21.9.76	1,304
D1044 Duchess	12.11.62	1.2.75	Collision damage at Oxford	Swindon 5.3.75	1,208
D1045 Viscount	16.11.62	16.12.74	Through wiring in very bad condition	Swindon 8.1.75	1,192
D1046 Marquis	24.12.62	11.12.75	Collision with 1064	Swindon 3.5.75	1,248
D1047 Lord	4.2.63	29.2.76	Planned withdrawal	Swindon 3.5.76	1,256
D1048 Lady	15.12.62	28.2.77	Planned withdrawal	Stored at N.A. 3.3.77. Sold: D. Rigby, Blackrod, Bolton	1,368
D1049 Monarch	14.12.62	26.4.76	Engine and transmission defects	Swindon 21.9.76	1,288

Locomotive	Built*	Withdrawn	Reason	Disposal†	Final Mileage (x 1,000)
D1050 Ruler	1.1.63	6.4.75	Waiting engines	Swindon 8.9.75	1,176
D1051 Ambassador	2.1.63	2.9.76	Full earth on through control circuits	Swindon 18.10.76	1,328
D1052 Viceroy	4.2.63	6.10.75	'A' end collision	Swindon 10.11.75	1,224
D1053 Patriarch	11.2.63	15.11.76	Engine defects	Swindon 5.1.77	1,304
D1054 Governor	2.3.63	25.11.76	Scrap tyres on 'B' end bogie	Swindon 4.1.77	1,336
D1055 Advocate	2.3.63	5.1.76	Severe collision damage at Worcester	Swindon 23.3.76	1,200
D1056 Sultan	8.3.63	15.12.76	Engine defects	Swindon 5.1.77	1,352
D1057 Chieftain	6.4.63	2.5.76	Planned withdrawal	Swindon 12.5.76	1,296
D1058 Nobleman	25.3.63	24.1.77	Dynostart fire	Swindon 24.3.77	1,312
D1059 Empire	6.4.63	6.10.75	Planned withdrawal	Swindon 10.11.75	1,216
D1060 Dominion	11.4.63	18.11.73	Waiting engines, due 'FX'	Swindon 14.3.74	1,032
D1061 Envoy	19.4.63	21.10.74	Waiting engines	Swindon 7.11.74	1,104
D1062 Courier	6.5.63	22.8.74	Waiting engines	Swindon 30.9.74 Then sold: Western Locomotive Assoc. 10/76	1.096
D1063 Monitor	17.5.63	4.4.76	Planned withdrawal	Swindon 23.9.76	1,184
D1064 Regent	24.5.63	11.12.75	Collision with 1046	Swindon 28.4.76	1,216
D1065 Consort	18.6.63	4.11.76	Planned withdrawal	Swindon 22.11.76	1,288
D1066 Prefect	14.6.63	12.11.74	Collision damage	Swindon 8.1.75	1,032
D1067 Druid	18.7.63	24.1.76	Planned withdrawal	Swindon 9.2.76	1,232
D1068 Reliance	12.7.63	12.10.76	'B' end final drive seized	Swindon 12.10.76	1,312
D1069 Vanguard	21.10.63	6.10.75	Planned withdrawal	Swindon 24.11.75	1,168
D1070 Gauntlet	28.10.63	30.12.76	'B' end collision damage	Swindon 24.3.77	1,312
D1071 Renown	7.11.63	7.12.76	'B' end final drive & cardan shaft seized	Swindon 23.2.77	1,232
D1072 Glory	7.11.63	2.11.76	Planned withdrawal	Swindon 26.1.77	1,280
D1073 Bulwark	3.12.63	29.8.74	Collision damage	Swindon 30.9.74	1,048

* Date Ex Works.   † Date of arrival at Swindon Works.

N.A. = Newton Abbot.
N.R.M. = National Railway Museum.

D1063 Western Monitor, *derelict at Laira 14th August 1976.*

Accidents

Perhaps the most severe incidents involving locomotives were those as follows:-

1. When D1040 *Western Queen* was involved in a fatal collision with a freight train on the 15th August 1963 at Knowle & Dorridge station when both driver and second man were killed.

2. Derailment of D1007 *Western Talisman* on the 19th December 1973 between Ealing Broadway and West Ealing, whilst heading the 17.18 eleven coach express from Paddington to Oxford. Ten passengers were killed and 53 injured in the accident.

3. Finally, when D1055 *Western Advocate* was severely damaged due to a collision on the 3rd January 1976 at Worcester Shrub Hill. Both driver and second man received fatal injuries whilst the engine was returning light to the West Country after delivering a clay train to Bescot yard.

D1007 Western Talisman

It was this locomotive which was involved in the Ealing derailment. An open battery-box door on the locomotive caused the accident, in which ten passengers were killed, the train being the 17.18 Paddington-Oxford on 19th December 1973. The door struck a "Limit-of-Shunt" signal at Old Oak Common, cable supports at Acton, then platform coping at Ealing Broadway station, which forced it downwards from its horizontal open position. Shortly afterwards it hit trackside machinery, so damaging a points motor as to force the train, travelling at 70 mph, to divert from the main to relief line at Longfield Crossover, the speed restriction for which is 25 mph

No.D1007 *Western Talisman* had been released from Old Oak depot after repairs at 14.00 the same day, and an unidentified fitter must have failed to lock the battery-box door, the London enquiry into the accident was told.

1977 – The Last Year

A complete withdrawal of the Westerns was expected within railway circles by the end of 1976. However, much to the surprise of many, seven still remained into the new year of 1977.

First of the 1977 condemnations was D1022 *Western Sentinel*. This locomotive was seen to be very popular amongst the Western enthusiasts during her final months of service. It frequently appeared on the 10.40 Paddington to Plymouth service which consisted of Mk II non air conditioned stock. This was one of the rare Western hauled passenger workings operating around that time.

The next Western withdrawal of 1977 was that of D1058 *Western Nobleman*, condemned on the 24th January due to a Dynostart fire. On the 23rd February, alas, D1041 *Western Prince* suffered a similar fate when her 'B' end Dynostart burnt out.

British Rail's final tour was now fixed for the 26th February and there were now only four locomotives left in running service. D1023 *Western Fusilier* and D1013 *Western Ranger* were chosen to work the "Western Tribute" tour, whilst D1010 *Western Campaigner* and D1048 *Western Lady* were chosen to act as reserve engines. Final withdrawal took place of all four locomotives on the 28th February 1977 and all were subsequently secured for preservation.

D1010 Western Campaigner *at Newton Abbot stabling point, August 1976.*

The Magnificent Seven
(The last to remain in traffic in 1977)

D 1010	WESTERN CAMPAIGNER
D 1013	WESTERN RANGER
D 1022	WESTERN SENTINEL
D 1023	WESTERN FUSILIER
D 1041	WESTERN PRINCE
D 1048	WESTERN LADY
D 1058	WESTERN NOBLEMAN

D1010 WESTERN CAMPAIGNER

Built Swindon (SW LOT 450)	–	15.10.1962
Date to Traffic fitted with Automatic Warning System (DAWS) and Dual Brakes (DB)	–	1.12.1972
Livery on Entering Service	–	Maroon
Other Liveries	–	Rail Blue/Full Yellow Ends Preserved Livery: Standard Loco Green/ (re-named and num- bered D1035 *Western Yeoman*)

Depot Allocations:

10/62	81A	OLD OAK COMMON
1/64	84A	LAIRA
1/68	87E	LANDORE
11/68	84A	LAIRA
2/77		WITHDRAWN (LAIRA)

FINAL MILEAGE – 1,360,000 MILES

1010 *Western Campaigner* was the first Western to emerge from Swindon Works in maroon livery and supporting half yellow warning panels.

Campaigner was always known for being a fast runner and it held some of the best Western timings. One of her most notable performances was probably that of 7th May 1966 when it powered the famous Ian Allan special, non-stop from London to Penzance, breaking three records in one day. The facts and brief description of that run were as follows:-

Organisers:	Ian Allan Ltd
Locomotive:-	D1010 Western Campaigner
Load:-	6 coaches – 208 Tons
Driver:-	F.J. Boase of Laira Depot
Second Man:-	Percy Furneaux of Laira depot

Records made

London – Penzance	5 hrs. 13 min.
London – Plymouth	3 hr. 19 min.
Penzance – Plymouth	1 hr. 36 min.
Maximum speed attained on run:-	94 mph

1010 was chosen for the special by fitter-inspector Ken Freeman. His choice being on the advice of driver F.J. Boase, who had driven the locomotive earlier in the week on the "Cornish Riviera Express" to Paddington, and back again to Plymouth the following day. He knew from this run that the locomotive was in excellent running condition.

Driver Boase was chosen to drive the special on the grounds of his experience and first hand knowledge of the road. His second man was Percy Furneaux and both men travelled as passengers from Plymouth to Paddington the previous day in preparation for the event. The challenge was now that of man and his machine, versus the odds, for this was a classic record breaking combination. Driver Boase recalls the amazing fact that locomotives, although exact in every other detail, can differ so much and one can be so much better than another. 1010 was always his favourite of the class and he was always pleased to have her booked to him.

Campaigner was in BR maroon livery at that time, a colour much favoured by Western enthusiasts.

The following is a brief account of the record breaking run, given by Driver Boase.

"At 07.35 hrs on the morning of 7th May 1966, the six coach special of 208 tons left Paddington. On arrival at Slough the train reached 94 mph and at Curry Rivel 92 mph. However we kept to the 90 mph limit wherever possible. If a Western is driven in excess of the 90 mph limit, a locomotive overspeed could take place, causing an automatic application of the brakes. As the locomotive's initial design was only for a

"Portrait of a Western" is my title for this picture. D1010 makes a beautiful sight as it gleams in the winter sunlight of Westbury, 3rd January 1977.

maximum running speed of 90 mph, we had to be very careful to avoid this.

At Lavington we lost two minutes due to a permanent way speed restriction, and disaster almost jeopardized the mission at Stampford Peverell intermediate signal box. Here the signalman was displaying a red flag owing to a signal failure. We should have stopped! However I instructed my second man to lower his window as I felt sure the signalman would give us permission to pass, although the signal was still at danger and to our relief, he did. This had made us four minutes down on time at Exeter. However we managed to recover this and reached Plymouth in the record time for a passenger train of 3 hrs 19 mins.

The train was booked through Plymouth at 3 hrs 25 mins, the previous record being 3 hrs 28 mins. After crossing Brunel's Royal Albert Bridge I had to reduce speed because we were ahead of schedule and the Manchester train in front of us was running slightly late. This created a situation where we were having distant signals against us showing danger, making our journey all the more tricky as the whole idea of the trip was to reach Penzance non-stop, which we eventually did, two minutes ahead of schedule 12.48 – 5 hrs 13 mins total time taken for the 305 miles.

There had been crowds at practically every station along the route. The train was greeted at Penzance by hundreds of enthusiasts. The television cameras were there and also the Mayor and Mayoress, Alderman and Mrs. Arthur Beckerleg. I was recognised by many, for I was born at Ludgvan, just three miles from Penzance and well known to all as Jack Boase.

After signing many autographs I took 1010 to Longrock for refuelling and a check, prior to leaving again at 16.00 hrs. On the return leg we reached Plymouth at 17.36, total time for the 80 miles being 1 hr 36 mins; again a record for this journey."

D1010 Nameplate at Westbury, 1. January 1977.

Another potential hazard for the record breaking attempt was the 60 mph speed restriction in Cornwall, as on no occasion should a driver exceed this.

No. 1010 *Western Campaigner* last entered Swindon Works on 15th June 1972 for intermediate repair and fitting of dual brake equipment, re-entering service on 1st December 1972.

Another landmark in the life of 1010 was to be her much remembered part in the Wirral Railway Circle's "Great Briton Ltd", when on the night of 26th May 1974 she hauled the 15 coach train over the 305 mile journey from Paddington to Penzance in just 5 hrs 39 mins. The train arrived on time at Taunton, the net time for this leg being less than the 122 minute scheduled time of the "Golden Hind" with a limited load.

No. 1010 was also in the news when on 17th March 1975 she towed the steam locomotive No. 6229 *Duchess of Hamilton* from Taunton to Swindon Works where the latter underwent final restoration work before being exhibited at the National Railway Museum at York.

As her days became numbered, 1010 was chosen to work various railtours along with sister locos 1023 *Western Fusilier* and 1013 *Western*

The Royal Albert Bridge, Saltash, with Class 50 No. 50034 Furious *approaching.*

Driver F. J. Boase of Laira.

Ranger. She also became a candidate to represent the class at the National Railway Museum, the others being Nos. 1023 and 1013.

On 27th November 1976, 1010 worked the British Rail "Tour 52", followed by the "Western Requiem Relief" tour on 13th February 1977. Her final tour was to be the "Western Requiem" on 20th February 1977. Unfortunately on this occasion she developed an engine fault shortly after leaving Paddington. However, she valiantly hauled the train through to Cardiff where a Class 37 (No. 37179) took over as far as Pontypridd where 1023 *Western Fusilier* was waiting to continue the tour.

Finally, on 26th February 1977, 1010 was to join 1048 *Western Lady* as the reserve engines for the "Western Tribute Railtour". The locomotives preceded the special from Old Oak Common to Bristol and later followed it to Plymouth to cover any failure.

After official withdrawal, 1010 was put into store at Newton Abbot depot together with locomotives Nos. 1013, 1041 and 1048. Here they were offered for sale by tender by BR.

Foster Yeoman Ltd of Shepton Mallet, Somerset, took possession of 1010 which was now less name and number plates. The locomotive arrived at their Merehead Quarry on 6th July 1977, but was in a poor external condition.

1010's new proprietors have since housed the locomotive in a new shed, together with three of their shunting locomotives. Originally it was the new owner's intention to restore 1010 in latter day Rail Blue livery and fix the name and number plates of D1035 *"Western Yeoman"*. However on the 15th July 1984 it was noted re-adorned in green livery with non-authentic full yellow ends and marker light panel, the new guise being to commemorate the original D1035, now scrapped, which had featured predominantly in the Company's railway development including the hauling of their first train in July, 1969. 1010's new name and number plates were the originals off D1035 having being presented to Foster Yeoman Ltd by the Western Region of British Rail in 1975.

At the time of writing there were between 60 and 70 trains per week moving more than three million tons of roadstone per year from the East Somerset quarry.

The new D1035 *Western Yeoman* lay dormant at the Merehead Quarry until 17th May 1986 when an agreement had been reached between Foster Yeoman Limited and the Diesel & Electric Group. This was for the locomotive to be loaned to them for full restoration purposes at the Great Western Society's Didcot Railway Centre.

However this locomotive has not yet been adorned externally as her original sister D1035. D1035 was the first Crewe-built Western to display green livery with yellow panels in July 1962, and was a magnificent example of this fine livery. Let us hope in time that D1010, being the famous loco it is, will eventually be bestowed with this honour, instead of the current fictitious livery.

It is understood that the locomotive will be returning to Merehead Quarry during 1988.

D1010 Western Campaigner stabled at Newton Abbot, August 1976.

Notable Railtours
of D1010 Western Campaigner

Tour	Date	Organiser	Route
The Great Briton Ltd	24.5.74 to 27.5.74	Wirral Railway Circle	Crewe via Thurso, Edinburgh, Paddington, and Penzance
Tour 52	27.11.76	British Rail	Plymouth – Bristol – Birmingham – Oxford – Basingstoke – Salisbury – Exeter – Plymouth
Western Requiem Relief	13.2.77	Railway Pictorial Publications	Paddington – Swindon – Gloucester – Cardiff – Pontypridd – Merthyr – Pontypridd – Aberdare – Pontypridd – Cardiff – Gloucester – Swindon – Paddington.
Western Requiem	20.2.77	Railway Pictorial Publications	Paddington – Swindon – Gloucester – Cardiff.

D1013 WESTERN RANGER

Built Swindon (SW LOT 450)   – 13.12.62
Date to Traffic fitted with
Automatic Warning System
(DAWS) and Dual Brakes
(DB)   – 14.1.72
Livery on Entering Service   – Maroon
Other Liveries   – Rail Blue/Full Yellow
    Ends
Preserved Livery   – Desert Sand
    (Displayed on the
    S.V.R. during 1980 for
    a short period only).
    Rail Blue/Full Yellow
    Ends

Depot allocations:

12/62	88A	CARDIFF CANTON
3/63	81A	OLD OAK COMMON
4/63	88A	CARDIFF CANTON
2/65	87E	LANDORE
2/66	86A	CARDIFF CANTON
4/66	84A	LAIRA
4/68	87E	LANDORE
10/71	84A	LAIRA
2/77		WITHDRAWN (LAIRA)

FINAL MILEAGE – 1,320,000

1013 *Western Ranger* first made the news on the 26th September 1965, when she was involved in an accident at Llanharan, whilst heading the 16.15 Swansea-Paddington service. The locomotive struck the tail of a crane when travelling at approx 35 mph due to a locomotive defect which had developed soon after leaving Swansea.

On 1st October 1971, 1013 last entered Swindon Works for an intermediate repair and fitting of dual brake equipment. It re-entered service with BR on 14th January 1972.

During 1975, *Ranger* made the limelight as a chosen exhibit way out west at St. Blazey Diesel Depot in Cornwall. The locomotive in immaculate condition was displayed before members of the Railway Division of the Institute of Mechanical Engineers, who were on a four day visit to Western Region territory.

Prior to the time of its most noted railtours 1013 spent most of her working life heading crack Western Region expresses and freight services, together with sister members of the class. Rosters took it from Paddington to South Wales, Paddington to Birkenhead, Paddington to Plymouth and Penzance, the same duties held as 'King' and 'Castle' class steam predecessors, but with improved timings. To name but a few, *Ranger* headed such named expresses as:-

"The Cornish Riviera Express", "The Mayflower", "The Bristolian", "The Golden Hind", "The Bristol Pullman" and "The Cornishman".

It also hauled heavy stone trains from Merehead Quarry in Somerset, clay liner services from Stoke Yard to St. Blazey and milk train services from St. Erth to Acton. 1013 together with sister members of the class was the mainstay of the Western Region services.

It was on 14th September 1975 *Ranger* worked her first railtour, for which duty she was now nominated. In immaculate condition it worked the "Bristolian-Tynesider" from Bristol to Birmingham and return; also on 25th October 1975 it hauled the Wirral Railway Circle's "Pembroke Coast Express".

The final year for the Westerns was officially 1976. On 1st May of that year, 1013 worked the "Severn Valley Flyer", this being the first tour when the locomotive was to be seen with its new, unique red name and number plates, a symbol of its tour status over the rest of the class and which was bestowed on her by British Rail.

On 22nd May 1013 hauled the 6000 Locomotive Association's "The

Previous page:

D1013 Western Ranger *prepare. to move forward at Bodmin Road Cornwall, 14th August 1976.*

48

D1013 Original BR nameplate but with red background. Seen here at Bodmin Road. This was the only Western to carry a red nameplate whilst in blue livery.

Merchant Venturer'' followed on 11th July by the Severnside Locomotive Association's "Torbay Explorer". The final tour of this individual glory was to be on 26th September when she was rostered for a British Rail tour from Paddington to Hereford, and return.

On 1st October 1970 sister locomotive *Western Fusilier* had just received a re-paint from Laira depot and been decreed from British Rail as a railtour locomotive. 1013 was now, after many months of railtour flagship, to share this honoured roll with 1023. However, on 13th November, 1976 1013 powered the Severnside Locomotive Association's "Cornishman" from Birmingham to Penzance and return.

20th January 1977 was to see 1013 on a most unusual working. It hauled the 07.30 service from Swansea to Leeds right through, as the locomotive originally booked had failed at Swansea prior to departure, leaving 1013 the only other motive power available. It was intended that the Western should work through to Birmingham or Derby where a replacement would be waiting to take over. However, no suitable substitute could be found at either location so the 52 was summoned to carry on, driven by the W.R. crew accompanied by an E.R. conductor. On arrival at Leeds 1013 made a rapid departure to Neville Hill for refuelling before returning south on the 14.43 Leeds to Plymouth service, which it worked throughout.

By this time, *Western Ranger* had become a choice for the National Railway Museum, together with sister locomotives, 1023 *Western Fusilier* and 1010 *Western Campaigner*.

On 19th February 1977, 1013 invaded the Southern Region with the Severnside Locomotive Association's "Southern Belle". This was to take the nine coach special through Bournemouth – Weymouth – Southampton – Guildford – Redhill – Reading and Ascot.

It was on 26th February 1977 that 1013 and sister locomotive 1023 *"Western Fusilier"* headed the British Rail "Western Tribute" railtour. It is perhaps for this, as with 1023, that she will be most remembered. As described earlier with 1023, both locomotives made rail history when they marked the end of the hydraulic era by setting out from London Paddington on the 630 mile journey to South Wales – Plymouth and return. It was the last time a Class 52 diesel hydraulic hauled train was to leave Paddington whilst in British Rail service.

No. 1013 was finally withdrawn from Laira on 28th February 1977, after working the "Western Tribute" railtour. Following withdrawal, 1013 together with Nos. 1010, 1041 and 1048 was put into store at Newton Abbot. There was considerable activity amongst the parties interested in their acquisition and a fair amount of liaison took place between them. However, despite the bargaining there was always the possibility of outside buyers tendering, of whom the former were not aware. Another unknown was that of the value B.R. would have placed on the locomotives. So even if one was successful in bidding against another there was no guarantee this would have been acceptable to B.R. To quote one potential buyer "It was a little like playing Russian Roulette".

Western Ranger was eventually tendered for and successfully purchased by R. Holdsworth Esq., on behalf of Holdsworth Conversions

Limited, a leading manufacturer of motor caravans. He, together with his advising party, Graham Howell and Phil Harper of the Western Locomotive Association had inspected all four locomotives before finally submitting his tender. Taking all into consideration the party thought it was by far the best locomotive available, though *Ranger* did have its problems (mainly in the profile of the tyres). However this was nothing that could not be taken care of, assuming that the various depots and workshops would be prepared to take on certain work. It was found *'Ranger'* had superior bodywork over the others and one very good engine. Unfortunately, the other engine had suffered rather long hours. Her two transmissions were good and also the electrics.

Western Ranger was finally purchased from British Rail in the spring of 1977, and was received by the new owners in the livery bestowed for her famous railtours, which was Rail Blue with full yellow ends, wheel rims painted white, and silver buffers. The actual sales acceptance form was signed on behalf of British Rail on 4th May 1977, by Mr. R.D. Read acting for the Director of Supply, British Railways Board, Derby.

The purchase price was less than £10,000 excluding name and number plates. These were offered to the general public and eventually sold for £1,134. The cost to restore 1013 as a working locomotive amounted to the same again as its purchase price, both in spares and British Rail workshops repairs. The locomotive now carries name and number plates made by a local model builder for a price of £300.

Richard Holdsworth actually took delivery of *'Ranger'* on behalf of his company in June 1977, when she was moved to Kingswear, on the Torbay and Dartmouth Railway. However the locomotive was not allowed to work under its own power so ironically, Class 47 No. 47013 was provided for towing purposes. Here she joined sister locomotive 1062 *Western Courier*.

Both locomotives were later transferred and are now in residence on the Severn Valley Railway at Bridgnorth.

D1013 Western Ranger *seen a Laira, August 1976. This locomo tive is now preserved privatel and under the care of Th Western Locomotive Association.*

It is the owner's intention to keep *'Ranger'* in British Rail blue with full yellow ends so that it would be the only preserved Western in such a livery.

Although 1013 is now permanently preserved and in safe keeping, the owner stresses his appreciation for the help given to him by the Western Locomotive Association and its members, without whom the preservation and operation of the locomotive would not have been possible.

The need for spares was recognised at an early stage if the locomotive was to be kept running for ten years or longer. Her owner provided the more major items and the WLA tendered at every opportunity to acquire spares from British Rail, and now has a fair reserve. It is with confidence that these items, together with the excellent facilities offered by the Severn Valley Railway, will enable the locomotive's custodians to undertake all but the most major operations.

Notable Railtours
of D1013 Western Ranger

Tour	Date	Organiser	Route
Bristolian-Tynesider	14.9.75	6000 Locomotive Association	Bristol – Birmingham – Sheffield – Newcastle and return.
Pembroke Coast Express	25.10.75	Wirral Railway Circle	Cardiff – Fishguard Harbour – Milford Haven – Pembroke Dock – Llanelli.
Severn Valley Flyer	1.5.76	Gwili Railway Company	Swansea – Cardiff – Gloucester – Worcester – Kidderminster and return.
The Merchant Venturer	22.5.76	6000 Locomotive Association	Bristol – Cheltenham – Birmingham and return.
Torbay Explorer	11.7.76	Severnside Locomotive Association	Severn Tunnel Junction – Bristol – Exeter – Paignton – Exeter – Westbury – Bristol – Gloucester.
Paddington – Hereford	26.9.76	British Rail	Paddington – Bath – Newport – Hereford – Worcester – Birmingham – Oxford – Paddington.
The Cornishman	13.11.76	Severnside Locomotive Association	Birmingham – Bristol – Exeter – Plymouth – Penzance and return.
Southern Belle	19.2.77	Severnside Locomotive Association	Waterloo – Bournemouth – Weymouth – Southampton – Havant – Guildford – Redhill – Guildford – Reading – Ascot – Waterloo.
Western Tribute	26.2.77	British Rail	Paddington – Swindon – Newport – Swansea – Newport – Bristol – Plymouth – Newbury – Paddington.

D1022 WESTERN SENTINEL

Built Swindon (SW LOT 450)   – 16.7.1963
Date to Traffic fitted with
Automatic Warning System
(DAWS) and Dual Brakes (DB) – 22.12.1972
Livery on Entering Service   – Maroon
Other Liveries   – Rail Blue/Full Yellow
                                    Ends

Depot Allocations:

7/63	81A	OLD OAK COMMON
9/63	86A	CARDIFF CANTON
2/65	87E	LANDORE
3/66	86A	CARDIFF CANTON
4/66	84A	LAIRA
1/77		WITHDRAWN (O.O.C.)

FINAL MILEAGE – 1,312,000

No. 1022 *Western Sentinel* was the first of the seven Westerns to survive through to 1977, to be withdrawn, being condemned on the 8th January 1977, due to derailment damage at Old Oak Common.

On entering service 1022 displayed the maroon livery of BR with black buffer beams and stocks, and half yellow warning panels each end.

During 1969, she was rostered for the "Cornish Riviera" and was logged by Ian Allan Ltd. for a "Train Running and Traction Performance" report. The following account is based on Mr. A. Wild's record of that event.

Sentinel headed a 13-coach train of 450 tons tare/480 tons gross, a load 40% heavier than the timetabled limit, for a horsepower output over 60 per cent greater. With the controller in the "fill" position, just before the "right a way" at Paddington, Notch 3 was used to start the train, on releasing the brakes. Notching up was then so rapid that full power was being applied before the last coach left the platform. The controller subsequently stayed in this position until the train reached Sonning Cutting. Upon clearance of the junction at Reading, power was then re-applied whilst the train accelerated nicely to Southcote Junction. Full power was again applied up the Kennet Valley, with the exception of an easing for the shortest distances possible, to conform to the numerous speed restrictions. Once again, full power was applied between Savernake and Patney. After Blatchbridge Junction it was Notch 9 with a vengeance up to Brewham. Brakes were applied for the curve above Bruton after which full power was used again down the valley, but with a brake application for Castle Cary.

The train reached Taunton in 113 min 56 sec; 4 min 44 sec inside the schedule time, and only 2 min 23 sec outside 1010 *Western Campaigner's* (6-coach load) record-breaking run. On the continuation to Exeter, Whiteball Summit was breasted, with two slowings to walking pace to pick up, and set down, a pilotman, because relaying required single line working near Cowley Bridge Junction. Exeter was finally reached in a net time of 148 min 13 sec, just 1 min 13 sec outside the schedule time for that journey. During her latter days "*Sentinel*" always appeared to be a slogger, and this occasion was no exception.

The table in Figure 1 makes an interesting comparison of the run with alternative motive power and different loadings. However, in comparing the run made by 1022, with say that of 1010 *Western Campaigner*, we must first consider the number of speed restrictions involved per run, of each locomotive. On the occasion of 1010 there were fourteen between Paddington and Exeter, compared with twelve encountered by 1022. In considering all the facts all the honours must surely go to her.

Sentinel last entered Swindon Works on the 24th April 1972 for fitting of dual braking equipment and intermediate repair, before being returned to traffic on the 22nd December 1972.

On the 27th September 1976, 1022 suffered an engine failure whilst hauling a 14 coach load annual special from Paddington to Exeter. The train had been chartered by the Exeter University Guild of students.

1022 Western Sentinel *storms* *way from Westbury, 3rd January 977 on the 10.40 ex Paddington-* *lymouth service. This is the one* *nd only picture I was ever able to* *ke of this locomotive. It was* *ithdrawn from service two* *eeks later, due to derailment* *amage at Old Oak Common.*

On the 30th October 1976 it was rostered from Exeter to the rescue of a failed Class 50 at Teignmouth. *Sentinel* powered the train to Dawlish, where it ran round and hauled the complete train from the front to Exeter.

On the 5th November 1976, the locomotive was commandeered to take over the 14.43 Leeds to Plymouth service, hauled by a 'Peak', which had caught fire at Gloucester. Fortunately, the local fire brigade managed to extinguish the blaze.

During her final weeks of service, 1022 became a martyr of the Class, and could be seen frequently heading the 10.40 am Paddington to Plymouth service, which by this time was one of the rare Western passenger workings.

Following withdrawal it lay derelict at Old Oak Common for several weeks until finally moved to Swindon for disposal on the 11th May 1977 where it was cut up on 14th December 1978.

Final Log of D1022 Western Sentinel

3.1.77	Worked 10.40 ex Paddington – Plymouth
7.1.77	Worked 10.40 ex Paddington, 12.17 ex Westbury – Plymouth
	Then worked a same day roster 16.07 to Bristol from Plymouth. Then returned to Laira on the 21.20 from Bristol for minor repairs.
15.1.77	07.45 service Llanelli parcels to Cardiff Canton then 18.30 Bristol to Paddington service.
16.1.77	Recorded on Old Oak Common depot prior to working 14.30 Paddington – Penzance service via Bath and Bristol.
17.1.77	Stabled at Penzance on hand, prior to working 16.40 Penzance – Acton milk service.
18.1.77	Stabled at Old Oak Common due to collision damage (damaged brake gear), and withdrawn.

Fig 1

RECORD BREAKING RUN OF 1010 6/280/220			819 AND 808 2 X 42 BB (4400) 9/321/345			1595 47 Co Co (2610) 9/320/345			1022 52 C-C (2700) 13/450/480		
	SCHED.	ACTUAL		SCHED.	ACTUAL		SCHED.	ACTUAL		SCHED.	ACTUAL
PADDINGTON			PADDINGTON			PADDINGTON			PADDINGTON		
TAUNTON	109m 30s	111m 33s	TAUNTON	113m	105m 17s	TAUNTON		111m 3s	TAUNTON	118m	113m 56s
EXETER	136m 30s	142m 32s	EXETER	139m	131m 34s	EXETER		137m 36s	EXETER	147m	148m 13s
TOTAL DISTANCE	173.50 MILES		TOTAL DISTANCE	173.50 MILES		TOTAL DISTANCE	173.50 MILES		TOTAL DISTANCE	173.50 MILES	
AVERAGE SPEED	76.26	73.02	AVERAGE SPEED	74.88	79.12	AVERAGE SPEED		75.67	AVERAGE SPEED	70.82	70.24

*D1023 Western Fusilier heads ea
out of Plymouth North Road on a
August evening of 1976.*

D1023 WESTERN FUSILIER

Built Swindon (SW LOT 450)	–	23.9.1963
Date to Traffic fitted with Automatic Warning System (DAWS) and Dual Brakes (DB)	–	13.9.1973
Livery on Entering Service	–	Maroon
Other Liveries	–	Rail Blue/Full Yellow Ends Preserved Livery: Maroon with small yellow panels

Depot Allocations:

9/63	86A	CARDIFF CANTON
2/65	87E	LANDORE
3/66	86A	CARDIFF CANTON
4/66	84A	LAIRA
2/77		WITHDRAWN (LAIRA)

FINAL MILEAGE – 1,256,000

Perhaps the most famous of all Westerns, No. 1023 started life early as a notable locomotive. During 1969 it was recorded powering a royal train through Newbury.

On 10th August 1972, it entered Swindon Works for an intermediate repair and fitting of dual brake equipment. Here it remained until 13th September 1973, and became the last Western ever to be returned to service from there.

It was on 6th April 1974 that it took part in a steam enthusiast special, hauling the "Western Mail Steam Special", before handing over to the steam locomotive No. 4472 *Flying Scotsman* at Newport.

Disaster struck on 29th January 1975, when 1023 ran derailed for 80 yards after having suffered a complete fracture of her leading axle whilst working the 14.05 Paddington to Birmingham express. Fortunately, the train was only travelling at 20 mph at the time.

1023 was next in the limelight on 20th April 1975, when it was noted as an official exhibit at Eastleigh on a British Rail Open Day.

On 27th April 1975, 1023 doubled headed 1051 *Western Ambassador* and worked the "Western Enterprise" railtour.

It was 1st October 1976 that saw 1023 with a new look. It had received a complete repaint at Laira depot and was noted as being a credit to the Western Region. This was the time that British Rail declared that 1023 would be the nominated locomotive to work specials. This formerly being the role of 1013 *Western Ranger,* which had for many months carried flagship status for the Western fleet. Also around this period in time, 1023 together with other possible choices, was being considered for preservation by the National Railway Museum at York. 1023 was now the pride of Laira and as a consequence received preferential treatment over the remaining fleet.

October 2nd, 1976 saw the locomotive run her first railtour sporting the immaculate new livery. This being the "Mercian Venturer" from Paddington to South Wales and was shortly followed by the "Western Sunset" special on 9th October 1976. No. 1023 was also summoned on the 23rd October 1976 for the British Rail organised "Tour 52".

On 30th October 1976, it worked the "Westerns South Western" railtour whilst double heading 1009 *Western Invader,* the latter being taken out of traffic only days later, due to the planned withdrawal by British Rail.

The following special was perhaps to be one of the most noted tours in rail history, when on 20th November 1976, 1023 was to invade the Eastern Region whilst working the "Western Talisman". The route took the locomotive from King's Cross to York and return. The crowds at York even exceeded those that witnessed a visit of the preserved LNER Pacific locomotive *Flying Scotsman* two years earlier! So dense were the crowds that the train had to be held on signals outside York whilst the track was cleared of sightseers who had overflowed from the platforms. It was on this tour that 1023 first displayed her new unique indicator blind panels for which she was to become known. Although *Fusilier* was the

D1023 Western Fusilier *passes Reading with the Cardiff-Paddington "Capitals United Express" on the 5th February 1977.*
(G. F. Gillham)

D1023 and D1013 Western Ranger *bring the "Western Tribute" railtour into Swansea High Street on the 26th February 1977.*
(G. F. Gillham)

first and only Western to appear at King's Cross, it was not, in fact, the first to appear on Eastern Region metals at York. York control recorded that during the early hours of 4th December 1974, Class 52, D1025 *Western Guardsman* had worked the Oxford – Middlesbrough car train there, returning immediately light engine. The following night, D1052 *Western Viceroy* had worked through as far as Rotherham on the same diagram.

The next tour was on 4th December 1976, when in partnership with 1056 *Western Sultan* it worked the "Western China Clay" from London to Plymouth and Falmouth.

1977 was the final year of the Westerns, and the first tour of the year was the "Western Memorial", headed by 1023.

By the end of January the choice for the National Railway Museum had narrowed to three; 1010 *Western Campaigner*, 1013 *Western Ranger* and 1023 *Western Fusilier*. The actual choice being delayed as long as possible due to the Museum especially requesting the chosen 52 to be in full working order.

On 5th February 1977, 1023 worked the "Capitals United Express" followed by the "Western Finale" railtour on 12th February 1977, as described in the Introduction. The next tour which followed was an unexpected one, for on 20th February 1977, the locomotive was to run light engine from London's Old Oak Common to Pontypridd where she was to pick up the ill fated "Western Requiem" railtour. On this 1010 *Western Campaigner* had suffered an engine failure and was declared "Failed" at Cardiff. A Class 37 (No. 37179) hauled the train from Cardiff to Pontypridd where 1023 powered it through to Merthyr before returning to Cardiff. This was a typical gesture on behalf of British Rail not to disappoint their devoted enthusiasts. No effort was spared by British Rail during the final months of the Western workings.

1023 together with 1013 *Western Ranger* will perhaps be remembered most for their part in the "Western Tribute" railtour. When, on the cold but sunny morning of 26th February 1977, both locomotives double heading paid final homage to the now erstwhile fleet. The 630 mile journey from Paddington to South Wales, Plymouth and return, was to take both locomotives through into rail history as they marked the end of the hydraulic era. As the special left Paddington it was watched by thousands. No more would a 52 be seen or heard leaving this famous Great Western station whilst in British Rail service.

This was the end of 1023 and 1013 as far as BR service went. It was the end of the remaining fleet, and in fact, the end of an era that will never be forgotten.

It was now known that 1023 had been chosen to represent the Class at the National Railway Museum. The decision being taken during the last week of service, on the advice of the Chief Mechanical and Electrical Engineer of the Western Region.

Finally, 1023 returned to Swindon, her original birthplace, prior to despatch for the National Collection. Whilst at Swindon it received no repairs or any kind of restoration works. On 15th December 1977, it left Swindon for the last time, destination Toton, en-route for York. Class 37 No. 37281 was provided for towing purposes as once diesel locomotives are withdrawn from British Rail service, they are banned from working under their own power anywhere on the network. The locomotive arrived in York in the same condition as withdrawn, though less name and number plates.

For several months the locomotive was a static exhibit at the NRM at York, having been restored to her original splendour of maroon livery with small yellow warning panels.

Since then 1023 has been loaned by the NRM to the Torbay & Dartmouth Railway (now Paignton & Dartmouth Steam Railway). A development proposed for the T&DR 1980 operating season was the use of *Western Fusilier* to work certain summer Saturday services. However, it failed an ultrasonic test on one of its axles earlier in that year and was unable to be delivered to Paignton as planned. However thanks to the Western Region authorities a replacement bogie was found and the locomotive arrived in Devon in time for the 1981 season.

Notable Railtours of D1023 Western Fusilier

Tour	Date	Organiser	Route
Western Mail Steam Special	6.4.74		
Western Enterprise	27.4.74	British Rail	Paddington – Bristol – Birmingham – Oxford – Reading – Paddington.
The Mercian Venturer	2.10.76	6000 Locomotive Assoc.	Paddington – Swindon – Newport – Hereford.
Western Sunset	9.10.76	Western Locomotive Assoc. and Gwili Railway Assoc.	Swansea – Cardiff – Bristol – Exeter – Plymouth and return
Tour 52	23.10.76	British Rail	Taunton – Bristol – Birmingham – Paddington – Newbury – Plymouth – Taunton
Westerns South Western	30.10.76	John Vaughan	Paddington – Newbury – Exeter – Meldon Quarry – Exeter – Yeovil Junction – Salisbury – Basingstoke – Reading – Paddington.
The Western Talisman	20.11.76	Western Locomotive Assoc.	King's Cross – Peterborough – Doncaster – York and return.
Western China Clay	4.12.76	John Vaughan	Paddington – Bristol – Plymouth – Truro – Falmouth – Truro – Par – Newquay – Par – Lostwithiel – Carne Point – Lostwithiel – Plymouth – Newbury – Reading – Paddington.
Capitals United Express	5.2.77	Monmouthshire Railway Soc.	Cardiff – Hereford – Worcester – Oxford – Paddington – Swindon – Gloucester – Newport – Cardiff
Western Finale	12.2.77	Peter Watts and Tony Fielding	Exeter – Bristol – Birmingham – Derby – Chesterfield – Leeds – York and return
Western Requiem	20.2.77	Railway Pictorial Publications	Pontypridd – Merthyr – Pontypridd – Cardiff – Bath – Swindon – Paddington.
Western Tribute	26.2.77	British Rail	Paddington – Swindon – Newport – Swansea – Newport – Bristol – Plymouth – Newbury – Paddington

D1041 Western Prince. *Driver T.F. Bradley of Trowbridge. Wilts. revs the engines at full throttle at Westbury depot, Wilts, 16th January 1977.*

D1041 WESTERN PRINCE

Built Crewe (DE LOT 286)	– 10.10.1962	
Date to Traffic fitted with Automatic Warning System (DAWS) and Dual Brakes (DB)	– 13.10.1969	
Livery on Entering Service	– Maroon/Yellow Buffer Beams and Stocks.	
Other Liveries	– Maroon/Small Yellow Panels/Full Yellow Ends. Rail Blue/Full Yellow Ends. Preserved Livery: Rail Blue/Full Yellow Ends, March 1985. February 1988 restored to original condition; Maroon/Yellow buffer beams and stocks.	

Depot Allocations:

10/62	81A	OLD OAK COMMON
3/63	88A	CARDIFF CANTON
9/63	81A	OLD OAK COMMON
1/64	82A	BRISTOL BATH ROAD
4/68	87E	LANDORE
11/68	84A	LAIRA
2/77		WITHDRAWN (LAIRA)

FINAL MILEAGE – 1,384,000

No. 1041 *Western Prince* was the third Crewe built Class 52 to be turned out in BR maroon livery, displaying full yellow buffer beams and stocks. However the latter were later painted black, as observed on 27th July 1963, when it was seen displaying the more familiar small yellow warning end patches, as was applied to the green liveried Westerns.

Some of *Prince's* early workings included that of the 12th October 1962, when it headed the 18.35 Paddington-Didcot semi-fast, and the following day was observed heading out of London, double heading a Type 3 'Hymek', No. 7010, on the "Pembroke Coast Express".

On 22nd January 1966 *Prince* was rostered for an unusual working. It headed the 18.10 service Paddington-Birkenhead, due to the failure of a Brush Type 4. *Prince* was summoned to continue the train to Shrewsbury, where it took over the 20.55 service Birkenhead – Paddington. However, owing to engineering works being in progress in Birmingham's Snow Hill Tunnel, the train was in fact terminated at Birmingham. 1041 then worked north again heading the 12.35 Birmingham – Chester special in lieu of the 09.25 Paddington – Chester which was terminated at Birmingham Moor Street.

The same year *Western Prince* was rostered for a most notable working, when on 3rd June it was bestowed the honour of a Royal Train duty during Her Majesty the Queen's visit to the West Country. *Prince* was seen in immaculate condition for the occasion, supporting maroon livery with yellow warning patches both ends.

No. 1041 last entered Swindon works on the 25th June 1969 for an intermediate repair and fitting of dual brake equipment. From here it was returned to traffic on the 13th October 1969, returning to its base depot Laira. It was from Laira that *Prince* was finally withdrawn on the 23rd February 1977 due to a failure of the Bend Dynostart and BR's planned programme of withdrawals.

At the time of withdrawal, 1041 *Western Prince* had recorded the second highest mileage of the Western fleet, only exceeded by 1005 *Western Venturer.*

After withdrawal the locomotive went into store at Newton Abbot diesel depot, together with locomotives 1010 *Western Campaigner,* 1048 *Western Lady* and 1013 *Western Ranger.* All of these being offered for sale by tender.

1041 was eventually bid for, and later successfully purchased on the 5th May 1977, by Mr. D. H. Edleston, a businessman of Osmaston Park Road, Derby. At the time of purchase, the locomotive was in a very shabby external condition, although this was to be a notable feature of it in latter BR days. The status won her the acclaim of thousands, plus the fact that it had run for 7^1/$_2$ years since the last major overhaul, without receiving any significant repairs – a most notable achievement by any standards, perhaps more so when one considers the high mileage this locomotive had covered. For this the accolade must surely go to 1041 as well as being a tribute to the men of Laira for their skill and never-ceasing efforts in maintaining the class during their final years.

After purchase the locomotive was examined by a BR inspector prior to removal to Swindon Works for fitting of a replacement 'B' end Dynostart. On examination the locomotive was found to have a damaged 'A' end intermediate final drive. This meant brackets having to be made to secure the drive pinion before the locomotive could be allowed to travel on the main line.

After all the necessary repairs had been carried out, 1041 together with 1048 *Western Lady,* was moved from Newton Abbot on the 28th June 1978 to Swindon Works. Both were hauled by two Class 31 locomotives, Nos 31135 and 31165. The convoy left Newton Abbot at 18.00 travelling overnight via Bristol Temple Meads, arriving at Swindon at 05.30 the following day. Whilst at Swindon 1041 also received attention to a faulty bogie, Dynostart, and various water leaks from both engines. The external appearance of *Prince* still left much to be desired, although the new owner confirmed that its bodywork was in sound condition.

1041 left Swindon Works in June 1980 travelling north via Derby to the BREL works at Horwich, Lancashire. At Derby the convoy was joined by preserved 'Warship' class No. D832 *Onslaught* before proceeding on the next leg to Horwich. On arrival both locomotives joined 1048 *Western Lady,* which had been stored there whilst under repossession by the Yates Burgess Finance Company.

All three locomotives were exhibited at the Works Open Day in August 1980, and were now officially under the care of a group called *Western Associates.*

It was the original intention of *Prince's* new owner to store the locomotive on the North Yorkshire Moors Railway at Grosmont, and have her repainted in the experimental golden ochre livery, once carried by 1015 *Western Champion*, complete with experimental 'T' warning sign. However both these intentions were later revoked; *Western Prince* arrived on the 11th February 1981 at the Bury Transport Museum in Lancashire, together with D832 *Onslaught*, where they are now permanent exhibits.

On arrival at the Bury Museum, *Prince* remained in its Rail Blue livery, but it has since been restored at BREL Crewe Works, including its original maroon livery with yellow buffer beams and stocks. The ultimate aim is now to see it commissioned for main line specials by tour operators.

D1041 Western Prince *is posed by* *driver E. Townsend at Laira* *before proceeding to the fuelling* *bay, 16th August 1976.*

D1048 WESTERN LADY

Built Crewe (DE LOT 286)   – 15.12.1962
Date to Traffic fitted with
Automatic Warning System
(DAWS) and Dual Brakes (DB) – 9.7.1970
Livery on Entering Service   – Maroon
Other Liveries   – Rail Blue/Full Yellow
                                Ends
                                Preserved Livery:
                                Standard Loco Green/
                                Small Yellow End
                                Panels

Depot Allocations:
12/62	88A	CARDIFF CANTON
12/62	82A	BRISTOL BATH ROAD
1/63	88A	CARDIFF CANTON
9/64	83A	NEWTON ABBOT
6/65	2/77	LAIRA
2/77	84A	WITHDRAWN (LAIRA)

FINAL MILEAGE – 1,368,000

No.1048 *Western Lady* was the first Western to receive full yellow ends in Rail Blue livery. BR decided to adopt this increased size warning panel on locomotive ends from 1968 onwards. In the case of the Class 52's this meant a complete painting of the front ends from the top of the buffer beams upwards including the cab window surrounds, all in yellow (see livery section for details).

Lady last entered Swindon Works on the 5th March 1970 for an intermediate repair and fitting of dual brake equipment. She was returned to traffic and her base depot Laira on the 9th July 1970. Plymouth, Laira became the final depot for all the class from December 1971 onwards.

During her later days *Lady* was frequently noted on stone train workings which initiated from Merehead Quarry near Shepton Mallet in Somerset. These were heavy workings inaugurated by 1035 *Western Yeoman,* which hauled the first official train of roadstone from the quarry depot in 1970. A duty subsequently shared by most of the Western fleet, but today performed by the American built Class 59s.

Perhaps the finest hour in the life of 1048 was on the 24th February 1977, when it was chosen to work the "Western Lament", the last privately organised railtour ever to be hauled by a Class 52 during BR service. It was also *Lady's* final appearance in BR service at the head of a passenger carrying train.

The locomotive attracted the usual atmosphere and excitement at Paddington to which Western specials were accustomed. The nine coach special left Paddington at 12.45 under rather dismal weather conditions. Adorned with headboard and wreath, the route was to take her through Newbury – Castle Cary – Westbury – Frome – Trowbridge – Swindon – Reading and return to Paddington.

Happily on this occasion there was sunshine after rain following such a dull start for both the locomotive and tour. On arrival at Castle Cary *Lady* ran around the train under brilliant sunshine, and the special began to shed its load. Suddenly there were shirt sleeves, camera clicks and commando type jumps appearing from everywhere! After the glamour, followed perhaps the saddest moment of the tour, when at Frome, John Vaughan the tour organiser, poured champagne down *Lady's* front end to mark the end of her reign!

On arrival at Paddington, 1048 came to rest at the Platform 2 blocks. It was all a bewilderment to both commuters, and interested onlookers. *Lady* was in her finality, and enjoying this unmarked individual attention of her fanatical followers. At 18.18 by Paddington's digital clock *Lady's* Maybachs began to roar. With a rapid succession of blasts from her horn it sped along the platform edge for the last time amidst loud cheers of defiance from her ardent admirers.

1048's final duty was on the 26th February 1977 when, together with 1010 *Western Campaigner* it acted as reserve engine for the BR

"Changing Crews" D1048 Western Lady heads an early morning stone train from Merehead Quarry into Westbury, 7th January 1977.

D1048 Western Lady *at Castle Cary on the "Western Lament" railtour 24th February 1977.*

(N. E. Preedy)

D1048 *at Frome on the "Western Lament".*

(N. E. Preedy)

organised "Western Tribute" railtour. The locomotives preceded the special to Bristol then followed it for the remainder of the journey back to Paddington.

On the 28th February 1048 *Western Lady* was finally withdrawn, and happily her forthcoming fate saved her from the scrapyard and breaker's torch. 1048 was the last Crewe built member of the class to remain in service with BR.

Eventually it was BR's decision to offer the locomotive for tender to the various preservation groups and individual buyers and on the 3rd March it went into store at Newton Abbot, together with its three surviving sister locomotives.

Western Lady was eventually tendered for and successfully purchased by, Mr. D. Rigby, of Blackrod, Bolton, Lancashire, who later placed the locomotive under the care of the North Yorkshire Moors Railway at Grosmont.

Together with 1041 *Western Prince* it was eventually moved on the 28th June 1978 from Newton Abbot to Swindon Works. Class 31 locomotives Nos 31135 and 31165 being provided for this operation. *Lady* remained at Swindon Works until 6th October 1978 in which period she received a bogie change and also had her name and number plates adorned with red backgrounds. It was 08.00 when 1048 left Swindon Works for the last time, bound for the NYMR.

Brush Class 31 No.31123, was provided for towing purposes on this next leg. The route took the locomotives through Stroud – Gloucester – Lickey Bank – Birmingham – Derby – Chesterfield – Sheffield and York. The convoy remained at Thornaby overnight and proceeded to Grosmont the following day.

Since arrival at Grosmont and under the ownership of D. Rigby, 1048 underwent major body repairs caused by damage sustained whilst in BR service. She also underwent a major face-lift by being adorned in Standard Green livery, an imitation of the BR livery, as applied initially to some of the first Crewe and Swindon built locomotives. A non-authentic livery of course for this particular member of the class. She also lost her original name and number plates and now carries replicas.

On the 18th March 1979 *Lady* was recalled from its North Yorkshire Moors residence to work the first Western railtour since the class was withdrawn by BR. The special was called the "Western Recall" and organised by John Vaughan it ran between Pickering and Goathland, a journey of approximately 28 miles total. 1048 later left the North Yorkshire Moors Railway at Grosmont due to difficulties with its new ownership. It was then repossessed by a finance company, Yates Burgess, and immediately stored at BREL Horwich Works. Here she remained whilst business transactions took place and it was an exhibit with 'Warship' No. D832 and 'Western' 1041 at the works open day in August 1980.

Again 1048 was offered for sale and was eventually purchased by a private preservation syndicate known as D1048 Western Lady Ltd., with a Mr. Ken Chinnock as its Managing Director and Chairman. However at the time of writing 1048 was still in store at Steamport, Southport in Lancashire awaiting possible removal to the West Country, which may or may not be the Plym Valley Railway.

D1048 at Westbury, January 1977.

D1058 WESTERN NOBLEMAN

Built Crewe (DE LOT 286)	– 25.3.1963	
Date to Traffic fitted with Automatic Warning System (DAWS) and Dual Brakes (DB)	– 15.2.1973	
Livery on entering Service	– Maroon	
Other Liveries	– Rail Blue/Full Yellow Ends	

Depot Allocations:

3/63	82A	BRISTOL BATH ROAD
6/63	88A	CARDIFF CANTON
3/64	87E	LANDORE
4/66	84A	LAIRA
1/77		WITHDRAWN (LAIRA)

FINAL MILEAGE – 1,384,000

Although 1058 *Western Nobleman* survived through to 1977, it was never chosen to work any of the famous railtours. However, during late August of 1965, *Nobleman* worked a C. J. Allen performance special, on the outward bound "Cornish Riviera Express", from Paddington to Plymouth, whilst sister locomotive 1045 *Western Viscount* worked the return leg.

Nobleman headed a 13 coach train of 443 tons tare (23 tons over the maximum for which this schedule was drawn up). On the footplate were Mr C. J. Allen, Driver Granger and Chief Locomotive Inspector Will Andress. The scheduled speed for the first leg of the journey to Taunton was a shade under 70 mph. With a gross load of 475 tons, it was apparent that *Nobleman* would have to be worked at full throttle for the major part of this distance. This meant an engine speed rising to 1,530 rpm max. when accelerating, but mostly an average of between 1,450 and 1,475 rpm which tends to be on the high side for one of these units. Slough was passed dead on time and a steady 80 mph was maintained on the level beyond Maidenhead. At Savernake the train was running one minute behind time due to a severe PW check at the east end of Reading station. However, with 3½ min recovery time and speeds of 83/88 mph through Pewsey and Patney the train passed through Lavington two minutes early. *Nobleman* maintained an average 82 mph through Heywood Road Junction and was now one minute inside the schedule. The highest speed of the journey so far attained was 88 mph at Pewsey which was again repeated at Curry Rivel *Nobleman* arrived at Taunton 34 seconds over the stated schedule owing to a severe PW check at Creech Junction.

At Taunton there was a change of crew allowing Driver Granger to return to London on the 'up' "Limited". With the departure of Driver Granger, the party was then joined by Driver Faulker before proceeding on the next leg to Exeter. Despite a PW slowing between Tiverton Junction and Cullompton, a 3½ minute recovery time and speeds of 80 mph through Stoke Canon more than put matters right, as Exeter was reached 1¼ minutes early, inside the stated 33 minutes schedule. This made a total time taken from Taunton of 31 minutes, net. On the final leg between Exeter and Plymouth, the scheduled allowance of 75 minutes included no less than an 8 minute recovery time. So with a punctual start from Exeter it would be difficult to be late. *Nobleman* and its 475 ton load rolled into Plymouth North Road, 3½ minutes ahead of schedule. This made the 225.55 miles from Paddington being covered in an overall time of 3 hr 65 min 17 secs gross, a net running time of 3 hr 40 min – an interesting feat to compare with the 4 hr non-stop schedules of their 'King' class steam predecessors and a clear indication of Western Region progress.

Nobleman last entered Swindon works on 24th May 1972 for intermediate repair and fitting of dual brake equipment. Whilst there, and in company with 1023 *Western Fusilier*, both locomotives became the last two Westerns ever to receive a major overhaul at these works.

On the 15th February 1973 *Nobleman* was returned to traffic newly finished in the standard livery of Rail Blue with full yellow ends.

D1058, in close-up at Old Oak Common, August 1976.

During January 1975 1058 was noted being hauled westward out of Exeter St. Davids, by sister loco 1053 *Western Patriarch*, presumed bound for Laira and final withdrawal. However, sightings at Paddington and Penzance two months later, during March happily proved this was not to be, and that it was still capable of performing top link services.

In its finality, *Nobleman* took on a very shabby appearance due to neglect and perhaps the later more frequent stone train workings from Merehead Quarry in Somerset. It survived until 24th January 1977 when finally withdrawn due to a Dynostart fire. Sadly 1058 arrived at Swindon for disposal on the 24th March 1977 and was subsequently cut up for scrap.

D1058 Western Nobleman *by th turntable at Old Oak Commo depot, London, 8th August 1976.*

The other side of D1058, Augu 1976.

August 1976 to February 1977

By August 1976 there were twenty four Class 52 Westerns remaining in running service with British Rail. It is with these survivors that the core of this pictorial tribute to this class has been formed.

The 24 Westerns in Traffic from August 1976

D1001	WESTERN PATHFINDER
D1005	WESTERN VENTURER
D1009	WESTERN INVADER
D1010	WESTERN CAMPAIGNER
D1013	WESTERN RANGER
D1015	WESTERN CHAMPION
D1021	WESTERN CAVALIER
D1022	WESTERN SENTINEL
D1023	WESTERN FUSILIER
D1028	WESTERN HUSSAR
D1033	WESTERN TROOPER
D1036	WESTERN EMPEROR
D1041	WESTERN PRINCE
D1048	WESTERN LADY
D1051	WESTERN AMBASSADOR
D1053	WESTERN PATRIARCH
D1054	WESTERN GOVERNOR
D1056	WESTERN SULTAN
D1058	WESTERN NOBLEMAN
D1065	WESTERN CONSORT
D1068	WESTERN RELIANCE
D1070	WESTERN GAUNTLET
D1071	WESTERN RENOWN
D1072	WESTERN GLORY

1015 Western Champion, *D1054 Western Governor and D1001 Western Pathfinder seen here at Westbury en route to the breakers' yard at Swindon on 2nd January 1977.*

D1001 WESTERN PATHFINDER

BUILT: Swindon 12.2.1962 (SW LOT 450)

LIVERY:
1. On entering service:-
   Maroon with yellow buffer beams and stocks, also white window frame surrounds.
2. From late 1962:-
   Maroon with half yellow warning panels.
3. From 1968:-
   Maroon with full yellow ends.
4. Between 1967 and 1971 onwards:-
   Rail Blue with full yellow ends.

DEPOT ALLOCATIONS:-

FEB 1962	–	83D LAIRA
OCT 1962	–	81A OLD OAK COMMON
MAR 1964	–	84A LAIRA
JAN 1968	–	87E LANDORE
FEB 1970	–	84A LAIRA

WITHDRAWN:-   4.10.1976
Reason:-   'B' end collision damage
Mileage:-   1,264,000
Disposal:-   Swindon 4.1.1977

Notable Events:

1967
Ran into the back of the 11.45 Paddington-Bristol service at Bristol, whilst at the head of the 12.00 Paddington-Swansea service.

1975
April 20th shared a special train working with 9F 2-10-0 No. 92203 *Black Prince*. The 14 coach special organised by the East Somerset Railway at Cranmore was bound for Eastleigh where locomotive D1023 *Western Fusilier* was an exhibit.

1976
Suffered collision damage at Stoke Canon with a BR van which proved fatal to the van driver. The locomotive was immediately withdrawn and ceased to become a possible preservation bid by Modern Traction Kits due to the damage sustained in the accident.

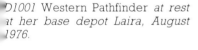

D1001 Western Pathfinder *at rest at her base depot Laira, August 1976.*

D1001 stabled at Exeter, 13th August 1976.

D1005 WESTERN VENTURER

BUILT:-   Swindon 18.6.1962 (SW LOT 450)

LIVERY: 1. On entering service:-
            Maroon with yellow buffer beam and stocks.
            2. Late 1962:-
            Maroon with black buffer beams and stocks and half yellow
            warning panels.
            3. Between 1967 and 1971 onwards:-
            Rail Blue with full yellow ends.

DEPOT ALLOCATIONS:-
JUN 1962   –   83D LAIRA
OCT 1962   –   81A OLD OAK COMMON
MAR 1964   –   84A LAIRA
JAN 1968   –   87E LANDORE
MAR 1969   –   84A LAIRA

WITHDRAWN:- 16.11.1976
Reason:-   'A' end Dynostart and cables burnt.
Mileage:-   1,392,000
Disposal:-   Swindon 5.1.1977

Notable Events:

D1005 *Western Venturer* held the highest recorded mileage of the Western fleet.

1962

On 12th December it ploughed into a herd of cows whilst travelling at approximately 75 mph working an express from Paddington and tackling the rising grade south of Cropredy. (Six cows were killed in the accident.) The locomotive suffered damage to the brake gear and was removed from the train at Banbury.

About this time *Venturer* was repainted in BR maroon livery with yellow buffer beam and stocks.

1963

It was recorded in the January edition of Modern Railways that her yellow buffer beams and stocks had been painted black and had received large yellow warning panels to her 'A' and 'B' ends.

1973

As from 2nd July 1973, 52s were booked to work the 06.53 Paddington to Birmingham New Street service and the 10.25 return via Oxford. D1005 was the first 52 to be rostered for this duty.

On 22nd September it was booked to work the diesel hauled portion of the ''Atlantic Venturers Express' between Plymouth and Newport. A role shared by preserved steam locomotives *King George V* and *Flying Scotsman*, *Venturer* had received special grooming at Laira for the event extending to whitened wheel rims.

1976

Sadly, 1005 was withdrawn from service on the 16th November due to the 'A' end Dynostarter cables being burnt in a fire. At the time of withdrawal the locomotive had travelled a total of 1,392,000 miles, a record which was never surpassed by any other Western whilst in BR service.

Arriving at Swindon for disposal on 5th January 1977 it was cut up on 17th June.

D1005 Western Venturer *leaving Plymouth on a mixed freight duty, early evening 13th August 1976. This locomotive holds the highest recorded mileage of the Western fleet.*

D1009 WESTERN INVADER

BUILT:-   Swindon 24.9.1962 (SW LOT 450)

LIVERY:-   1. On entering service:-
              Maroon with yellow buffer beams and stocks.
           2. Late 1962 – Early 1963:-
              Maroon with black buffer beams and stocks and half yellow
              warning panel
           3. Between 1967 and 1971 onwards:-
              Rail Blue with full yellow ends.

DEPOT ALLOCATIONS:-
SEPT 1962   –   81A OLD OAK COMMON
FEB 1964   –   84A LAIRA
JAN 1968   –   87E LANDORE
DEC 1968   –   84A LAIRA
MAR 1970   –   87A LANDORE
OCT 1971   –   84A LAIRA

WITHDRAWN:- 10.11.1976
Reason:-   Planned withdrawal, ie. broken bogie spring and fractured
             steam pipe.
Mileage;-   1,376,000
Disposal:-   Locomotive offered for tender in full working order except for
             the above defects. After no successful tenders were accepted
             for preservation, the engines and cooler were removed and
             sold to a Dutch scrap dealer during May 1977. On 1.6.77 the
             remains arrived at Swindon, and have since been cut up.

Notable Events:

1976
September 5th worked a return special organised by Modern Traction Kits from
Paddington to Eastleigh and return.

     October 30th worked the John Vaughan "Westerns South Western" railtour
whilst double heading D1023 *Western Fusilier* from Paddington to Meldon
Quarry and return via Exeter – Yeovil Junction – Salisbury – Basingstoke and
Reading.

D1010 WESTERN CAMPAIGNER

BUILT:-   Swindon 15.10.1962 (SW LOT 450)

LIVERY: 1. On entering service:-
              Maroon with half yellow warning panels. (This was the first
              Swindon built locomotive to carry that livery).
           2. Between 1967 and 1971 onwards:-
              Rail Blue with full yellow ends.

DEPOT ALLOCATIONS:-
OCT 1962   –   81A OLD OAK COMMON
JAN 1964   –   84A LAIRA
JAN 1968   –   87E LANDORE
NOV 1968   –   84A LAIRA

WITHDRAWN:- 28.2.1977
Reason:-   Planned withdrawal
Mileage:-   1,360,000
Disposal:-   Newton Abbot 3.3.1977

PRESERVATION STATUS:-
Privately owned by:-   Foster Yeoman Limited,
                         East Cranmore,
                         Shepton Mallet
                         Somerset.

Under the care of:-
1. The above
2. On loan to the Diesel and Electric Group at the Great Western Society's Didcot
   Railway Centre.

D1009 Western Invader *looking
immaculate leaves Exeter St. Davids bound for Paddington, 13th
August 1976.*

PRESERVED LIVERY:-
1. Original Rail Blue D1010 with full yellow ends.
2. Standard Loco Green/full yellow ends and marker lights panel. Named and numbered D1035 Western Yeoman.
3. Standard Loco Green throughout with red buffer beams and stocks plus BR embossed crest.

Notable Events:

1966
May worked an Ian Allan Ltd special, breaking three records in one day.

1974
May took part in the Wirral Railway Circle's "Great Briton Ltd".

1975
March – Towed steam locomotive 6229 Duchess of Hamilton from Taunton to Swindon works.

1976
November worked British Rail's "Tour 52".

1977
February   1. Worked the "Western Requiem Relief"
            2. Worked the "Western Requiem"
            3. Acted as reserve engine together with D1048 for the "Western Tribute" railtour.

D1010 on a frosty morning at Westbury, January 1977.

D1010 Western Campaigner *waits her next turn of duty at Newton Abbot stabling point, August 1976.*

D1013 WESTERN RANGER

BUILT:- Swindon 13.12.1962 (SW LOT 450)

LIVERY:- 1. On entering service:-
            Maroon with half yellow warning panels.
          2. Between 1967 and 1971 onwards:-
            Rail Blue with full yellow ends.

DEPOT ALLOCATIONS:-

DEC 1962	–	88A CARDIFF CANTON
MAR 1963	–	81A OLD OAK COMMON
APR 1963	–	88A CARDIFF CANTON
FEB 1965	–	87E LANDORE
FEB 1966	–	86A CARDIFF CANTON
APR 1966	–	84A LAIRA
APR 1968	–	87E LANDORE
OCT 1971	–	84A LAIRA

WITHDRAWN:- 28.2.1977
Reason:-   Planned withdrawal
Mileage:-   1,320,000
Disposal:-   Newton Abbot 3.3.1977

PRESERVATION STATUS:-
Privately owned by:-   Richard Holdsworth Esq.
                       Holdsworth Conversions Ltd.
                       London Bridge Road, Woodley, Reading, Berks.
Under the care of:-   The Western Locomotive Association,
                       Severn Valley Railway, Bridgnorth

PRESERVED LIVERY:-
1. Rail Blue with full yellow ends.
2. Desert Sand
3. Rail Blue with full yellow ends.

Notable Events:

1965
September accident at Llanharan.

1975
An exhibit at St. Blazey diesel depot.
Became railtour locomotive as described earlier.

D1015 WESTERN CHAMPION

BUILT:- Swindon 21.1.1963 (SW LOT 450)

LIVERY:- 1. On entering service:-
            Golden Ochre with experimental yellow warning panels. Also
            Golden Ochre buffer beams and window surrounds.
          2. From 1965:-
            Maroon with half yellow warning panels.
          3. Between 1967 and 1971 onwards:-
            Rail Blue with full yellow ends.

DEPOT ALLOCATIONS:-

JAN 1963	–	88A CARDIFF CANTON
MAR 1963	–	81A OLD OAK COMMON
JUN 1963	–	88A CARDIFF CANTON
SEPT 1963	–	81A OLD OAK COMMON
FEB 1964	–	84A LAIRA
NOV 1968	–	87E LANDORE
OCT 1971	–	84A LAIRA

WITHDRAWN:- 13.12.1976
Reason:-   Derailment Damage
Mileage:-   1,296,000
Disposal:-   Swindon 4.1.1977

D1013 Western Ranger seen leaving Bodmin Road on a train bound for London Paddington, August 1976.

PRESERVATION STATUS:-
Privately owned by: The Diesel Traction Group
Under the care of: BR Swindon Works

PRESERVED LIVERY:-   Golden Ochre, as carried in the early 1960s.

Notable Events:

1965
Famous for hauling the returning empty stock of Pullmans which formed Winston Churchill's funeral train during 1965.

Champion, built at Swindon in January 1963 was also a unique member of the class due to the experimental livery of Golden Ochre. (A precise match to that of the preserved Stroudley 'Terriers'). It was also the only member of the class to sport the experimental 'T' yellow warning panel at her 'B' end, and a modified half yellow warning panel at the 'A' end.

The locomotive was repainted maroon in 1965 and later Rail Blue with full yellow ends as with the rest of the class.

On 29th October 1965 it worked the north bound "Devonian" through to Derby.

1976
Champion was finally withdrawn on the 13th December, due to derailment damage at Castle Cary in which it sustained a ruptured fuel tank.

1977
1015 arrived at Swindon for disposal on the 4th January with 1,296,000 miles on the clock. It had been towed there from the West Country in company with 1054 *Western Governor* and 1001 *Western Pathfinder.* Following arrival at Swindon it was revealed at one stage by BR that the locomotive might escape the breaker's torch, and be held as an example of the Work's products, similar to 'Warship' class locomotive No. 818.

However the locomotive was later offered for tender and purchased by The Diesel Traction Group. At that time all the major components of 1015 were in situ, but one of her engines had been cannibalised. Also, the name and number plates, A.W.S. equipment and various items of brake gear had been removed.

However since purchase the locomotive has remained at Swindon Works and in 1982 was noted restored to the unique Golden Ochre livery as carried in the early 1960s.

Presently stored under cover inside the former DMU Repair Shop at Swindon Works, where it is hoped to set up a Heritage Centre. It is still in Golden Ochre livery with the experimental yellow 'T' panel.

Mechanically, one engine failed very badly just after the Old Oak Common Open Day in 1985. A spare engine is at present being rebuilt which, when finished will be lifted in to replace the defective one. Also a major overhaul is being carried out on all the electrical wiring in the driving cabs.

D1015 Western Champion *at Laira, August 1976. This locomotive pulled the returning empty stock of Sir Winston Churchill's funeral train and was the only Western painted golden ochre. The end came due to a derailment at Castle Cary where it suffered a fractured fuel tank.*

D1021 WESTERN CAVALIER

BUILT: Swindon 17.6.1963 (SW LOT 450)

LIVERY: 1. On entering service:-
              Maroon with half yellow panel.
           2. Between 1967–1971 onwards:-
              Rail Blue with full yellow ends.

DEPOT ALLOCATIONS:-
JUNE 1963   –   81A OLD OAK COMMON
SEPT 1963   –   86A CARDIFF CANTON
JUNE 1964   –   82A BRISTOL BATH ROAD
MAR 1969   –   84A LAIRA

WITHDRAWN:- 10.8.1976
Reason:-   Collision damage
Mileage:-   1,280,000
Disposal:-   Swindon 23.9.1976

Notable Facts:
Name and number plates were displayed in BREL Swindon Works offices.

D1022 WESTERN SENTINEL

BUILT: Swindon 16.7.1963 (SW LOT 450)

LIVERY: 1. On entering service:-
              Maroon with half yellow warning panels.
           2. Between 1967 and 1971 onwards:-
              Rail Blue with full yellow ends.

DEPOT ALLOCATIONS:-
JUL 1963   –   81A OLD OAK COMMON
SEP 1963   –   86A CARDIFF CANTON
FEB 1965   –   87E LANDORE
MAR 1966   –   86A CARDIFF CANTON
APR 1966   –   84A LAIRA

WITHDRAWN:- 18.1.1977
Reason:-   Derailment damage at O.O.C.
Mileage:-   1,312,000
Disposal:-   Swindon 11.5.1977

D1021 Western Cavalier *passes through Dawlish with the 08.40 Penzance-Paddington on the 2nd August 1975.*
(G. F. Gillham)

D1022 Western Sentinel *at St. Budeaux Junction, Plymouth on 5th June 1974 with train 1V.72 the 7.08 Bradford-Penzance.*
(N.E. Preedy)

D1023 WESTERN FUSILIER

BUILT:-   Swindon 23.9.1963 (SW LOT 450)

LIVERY:-   1. On entering service:-
           Maroon with half yellow warning panels.
       2. Between 1967 and 1971 onwards:-
           Rail Blue with full yellow ends.

DEPOT ALLOCATIONS:-

SEPT 1963	–	86A CARDIFF CANTON
FEB 1965	–	87E LANDORE
MAR 1966	–	86A CARDIFF CANTON
APR 1966	–	84A LAIRA

WITHDRAWN:- 28.2.1977
Reason:-   Planned withdrawal
Mileage:-   1,256,000
Disposal:-   N.R.M. 27.2.77

PRESERVATION STATUS:-
Owners: National Railway Museum
              Leeman Road
              York
Under the   Paignton & Dartmouth
care of: Steam Railway

PRESERVED LIVERY:-   Maroon with half yellow warning panels.

Notable Events:

1969
Royal Train working.

1973
Last Western ever to receive a major overhaul in
Swindon Works.

1974
Worked the "Western Mail Steam Special".

1975
Derailed working Paddington to Birmingham
express.
Exhibited at Eastleigh.
Worked the "Western Enterprise" railtour.

1976
Declared railtour locomotive. (See previous list of
trains worked).
First Western to invade the Eastern Region at King's
Cross.
Became the only Western to display indicator blind
panels.

(Other facts of interest regarding this locomotive
are as described earlier in this book.)

D1028 WESTERN HUSSAR

BUILT: Swindon 25.2.1964 (SW LOT 450)

LIVERY: 1. On entering service:-
               Maroon with half yellow warning panel.
            2. Between 1967–1971 onwards:-
               Rail Blue with full yellow ends.

DEPOT ALLOCATIONS:-
FEB 1964   –   82A BRISTOL BATH ROAD
JUNE 1969   –   84A LAIRA

WITHDRAWN:- 6.10.1976
Reason:-   Collision damage
Mileage:-   1,256,000
Disposal:-   Swindon 18.10.1976

D1033 Western Trooper *leaving Exeter St. Davids heading eastward for Paddington, 13th August 1976.*

D1028 at Laira, 18th August 1976.

D1033 WESTERN TROOPER

BUILT: Crewe 17.1.1964 (DE LOT 286)

LIVERY: 1. On entering service:-
                Maroon with half yellow panel.
             2. Between 1967–1971 onwards:-
                Rail Blue with full yellow ends.

DEPOT ALLOCATIONS:-
JAN 1964   –   81A OLD OAK COMMON
MAR 1964   –   83A NEWTON ABBOT
JUNE 1965   –   84A LAIRA

WITHDRAWN:-   17.9.1976
Reason:-   Worn tyre on 'B' end bogie
Mileage:-   1,272,000
Disposal:-   Used as a train heating unit at Laira depot. Later, engines were
                 removed and locomotive cannibalised. Remains arrived at
                 Swindon for disposal on the 24.3.1977.

D1036 WESTERN EMPEROR

BUILT:-   Crewe 29.8.1962 (DE LOT 286)

LIVERY:-   1. On entering service:-
                Standard locomotive green with half yellow warning panels.
             2. From approx. 1966:-
                Experimental Blue with half yellow warning panels.
             3. Between 1967 and 1971 onwards:-
                Rail Blue with full yellow ends.

DEPOT ALLOCATIONS:-
AUG 1962   –   83D LAIRA
OCT 1962   –   81A OLD OAK COMMON
JAN 1966   –   84A LAIRA

WITHDRAWN:-   1.11.1976
Reason:-   Planned withdrawal
Mileage:-   1,360,000
Disposal:-   Swindon 22.11.1976

*D1036 Western Emperor passe.
the closed station at Patney &
Chirton with the 06.35 Penzance
Paddington on the 31st March
1975.*

(G. F. Gillham

Notable Events:

1975
March 29th worked the outward run of the Plymouth Railway Circle and Wirral
Railway Circle's special from Plymouth to Derby, together with sister locomotive
D1052 *Western Viceroy. Emperor* worked the special as far as Westbury on the
outward run. It then proceeded light engine to Bristol ready for the return
working to Plymouth.

Note:
The number plates were set at a higher position than on other members of the
class.

D1036 at Laira, 18th August 1976.

D1041 WESTERN PRINCE

BUILT: Crewe 10.10.1962 (DE LOT 286)

LIVERY: 1. On entering service:-
          Maroon with yellow buffer beams and stocks.
        2. Late 1962 – Early 1963:-
          Maroon with black buffer beams and stocks and half yellow
          warning panels.
        3. From approx. 1968:-
          Maroon with full yellow panels.
        4. Between 1967 and 1971 onwards:-
          Rail Blue with full yellow panels.

DEPOT ALLOCATIONS:-

OCT 1962	–	81A OLD OAK COMMON
MAR 1963	–	88A CARDIFF CANTON
SEP 1963	–	81A OLD OAK COMMON
JAN 1964	–	82A BRISTOL BATH ROAD
APR 1968	–	87E LANDORE
NOV 1968	–	84A LAIRA

WITHDRAWN:-   23.2.1977
Reason:-   'B' end Dynostart burnt out.
Mileage:-   1,384,000
Disposal:-   Newton Abbot 25.2.1977

PRESERVATION STATUS:-
Privately owned by:-   D.H. Edleston, Derby.
Under the care of:-   The Bury Transport Museum, Lancashire.

PRESERVED LIVERY:-
1. Rail Blue with full yellow ends
2. Original Maroon with yellow buffer beams and stocks.

Notable Events:

1966
June 3rd. Royal Train working H.M. The Queen to West Country.

1987
At the end of June D1041 returned in the early hours to its original birthplace, Crewe Locomotive Works. It was a chosen exhibit for the Annual Works Open Day on 4th July and later the Crewe Heritage celebrations between 4th July and the 16th August, an event which was later to be screened in the form of a documentary on BBC2 Television and in Video *Railscene 12.*

It was due to the enthusiasm of *Prince's* owner, Mr. D.H. Edleston of Derby, which initiated the appearance of the diesel hydraulic at this prestigious event. For immediately Mr. Edleston was to learn of the celebrations, he approached officials at Crewe offering the loan of his locomotive for exhibition.

Following an official inspection at Bury by the B.R. respresentatives, the locomotive was officially booked to appear, complete with a special invitation for its owner to be present for a visit by Her Majesty the Queen and the Duke of Edinburgh.

The great day was on 24th July 1987, the official opening day and visit by Her Majesty to the Heritage Festival. D1041 was exhibited together with No. 71000 *Duke of Gloucester,* No. 6201 *Princess Elizabeth,* Class 24 No. 5054, *Cornwall* and Class 8F No. 48151 from the Midland Railway Centre.

Previously, *Prince's* owner had felt uneasy about the shabby exterior of his locomotive for such an occasion. However the proud moment arrived for Mr. Edleston when the Queen, accompanied by the Mayor of Crewe and Nantwich, and Prince Philip approached his locomotive. The Queen asked, "Is this a preserved locomotive already?" Mr. Edleston replied, "Yes, Your Majesty, I've had the locomotive for ten years now". The Duke of Edinburgh then enquired, "Where do you keep a thing like this?" to which Mr. Edleston answered, "It's normally kept on the East Lancashire Preserved Railway at Bury, where it runs on a private stretch of line and is a major tourist attraction there for enthusiasts at weekends." Mr. Edleston went on to say he was hoping to have it repainted after the exhibition in the original maroon livery of British Rail.

"Well, it would look better than it does now," replied the Duke...

At the time of writing, despite the financial burden to its owner, *Prince* is undergoing full body restoration and repainting at BREL Crewe locomotive works. This is therefore the only preserved Western to be restored externally to her original magnificence in a British Railways' workshop.

D1041 at Westbury depot, 15th January 1977.

D1041 Western Prince *passe[s]
Westbury, 17th January 1977.*

*The proud owner of D104[1]
Western Prince Mr. D. H. Edlesto[n]
meets Her Majesty the Queen an[d]
Prince Philip at the formal opening
of the Crewe Heritage Centre
24th July 1987.*
   (Courtesy Chester Chronicle[)]

*D1048 at Westbury, 9th Januar[y]
1977.*

D1048 WESTERN LADY

BUILT:-   Crewe 15.12.1962 (DE LOT 286)

LIVERY:-   1. On entering service:-
        Maroon with half yellow warning panels.
      2. Between 1967 and 1971 onwards:-
        Rail Blue with full yellow ends. (D1408 was the first in this livery).

DEPOT ALLOCATIONS:-

DEC 1962	–	88A CARDIFF CANTON
DEC 1962	–	82A BRISTOL BATH ROAD
JAN 1963	–	88A CARDIFF CANTON
SEP 1964	–	83A NEWTON ABBOT
JUN 1965	–	84A LAIRA

WITHDRAWN:- 28.2.1977
Reason:-   Planned withdrawal
Mileage:-   1,368,000
Disposal:-   Newton Abbot 3.3.1977

PRESERVATION STATUS:-
Privately owned by:-   1. D. Rigby, Bolton.
                       2. Yates Burgess Finance Co.
                         (Repossession)
                       3. D1048 Western Lady Ltd.
                         (Mr. K. Chinnock & Syndicate)

Under the care of:-   1. The North Yorkshire Moors Railway, Grosmont
                       2. British Rail Engineering Ltd, Horwich
                       3. Steamport, Southport

Preserved Livery:-   Brunswick Green with half yellow panels and red
                       bufferbeams and stocks

Notable Events:

1977
February worked the last privately organised BR
railtour, the "Western Lament".
    Acted as reserve engine together with D1010
for the "Western Tribute" railtour.
1988
Transferred from Steamport to the West Country,
and appeared at BR Laira Open Day 17th July.

D1048 Western Lady *seen here in August 1976 at her base depot Laira, Plymouth. Again this locomotive was specially positioned for photography. D1048 is now preserved in green livery.*

D1051 WESTERN AMBASSADOR

BUILT: Crewe 2.1.1963 (DE LOT 286)

LIVERY: 1. On entering service:-
               Maroon with half yellow warning panels.
            2. Between 1967 and 1971:-
               Rail Blue with full yellow ends.

DEPOT ALLOCATIONS:-
JAN 1963   –   88A CARDIFF CANTON
SEPT 1963   –   81A OLD OAK COMMON
JAN 1964   –   84A LAIRA

WITHDRAWN:- 2.9.1976
Reason:-   Full earth on through control circuits.
Mileage:-   1,328,000
Disposal:-   Swindon 18.10.1976

Notable Events:

1975
Worked the "Western Enterprise" railtour on 27th April whilst double heading
D1023 *Western Fusilier*.

D1051 Western Ambassador
urries the 07.53 Paignton-
'addington through Slough on the
'0th May 1975.

(G. F. Gillham)

D1053 WESTERN PATRIACH

BUILT: Crewe 11.2.1963 (DE LOT 286)

LIVERY: 1. On entering service:-
              Maroon with half yellow panel.
          2. Between 1967 and 1971 onwards:-
              Rail Blue with full yellow ends.

DEPOT ALLOCATIONS:-
FEB 1963   –   81A OLD OAK COMMON
MAR 1963   –   88A CARDIFF CANTON
OCT 1963   –   81A OLD OAK COMMON
JAN 1964   –   82A BRISTOL BATH ROAD
MAY 1969   –   84A LAIRA

WITHDRAWN:- 15.11.1976
Reason:-   Engine defects
Mileage:-   1,304,000
Disposal:-   Swindon 5.1.1977

D1053 Western Patriarch *stabled at Plymouth North Road, 15th August 1976.*

D1053 glistens in the lovely afternoon sunshine at Laira depot. This locomotive appeared in excellent condition externally.

D1054 WESTERN GOVERNOR

BUILT: Crewe 2.3.1963 (DE LOT 286)

LIVERY: 1. On entering service:-
             Maroon with half yellow warning panel.
          2. From approx. 1968:-
             Maroon with full yellow panels.
          3. Between 1967 and 1971 onwards:-
             Rail Blue with full yellow ends.

DEPOT ALLOCATIONS:-
MAR 1963   –   88A CARDIFF CANTON
APR 1964   –   87E LANDORE
APR 1966   –   84A LAIRA

WITHDRAWN:- 25.11.1976

Reason:-   Bogie defects
Mileage:-   1,336,000
Disposal:-   Swindon 4.1.1977

D1054 Western Governor *enters
the fuelling bay at Laira.*

D1056 WESTERN SULTAN

BUILT: Crewe 8.3.1963 (DE LOT 286)

LIVERY:
1. On entering service:-
   Maroon with half yellow warning panels.
2. From approx. 1968:-
   Maroon with full yellow ends.
3. Between 1967 and 1971 onwards:-
   Rail Blue with full yellow ends.

DEPOT ALLOCATIONS:-

MAR 1963	–	88A CARDIFF CANTON
MAR 1964	–	87E LANDORE
APR 1966	–	84A LAIRA

WITHDRAWN:- 15.12.1976

Reason:-	Engine defects
Mileage:-	1,352,000
Disposal:-	Swindon 5.1.1977

Notable Events:

1976

December 4th worked the "Western China Clay" railtour in partnership with D1023 *Western Fusilier. Sultan* was attached to the rear of the special at Truro and worked with 1023 to Falmouth. It then headed the special back to Truro with 1023 trailing. The latter was detached at Truro whilst 1056 then headed the train to Par reversed.

From Par *Sultan* continued the special along the branch to Newquay. The locomotive then returned the special to Par, and subsequently worked east to Lostwithiel whilst 1023 then commandeered the special to Carne Point with 1056 at the rear. *Sultan* returned the train to Lostwithiel with 1023 trailing, the latter then being detached whilst 1056 headed the special back to Paddington via Plymouth.

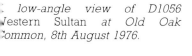

low-angle view of D1056 Western Sultan at Old Oak Common, 8th August 1976.

D1058 WESTERN NOBLEMAN

BUILT:-   Crewe 25.3.1963 (DE LOT 286)

LIVERY:-   1. On entering service:-
              Maroon with half yellow warning panel.
           2. Between 1967 and 1971 onwards:-
              Rail Blue with full yellow ends.

DEPOT ALLOCATIONS:-
MAR 1963   –   82A BRISTOL BATH ROAD
JUN 1963   –   88A CARDIFF CANTON
MAR 1964   –   87E LANDORE
APR 1966   –   84A LAIRA

WITHDRAWN:- 24.1.1977
Reason:-   Dynostart fire
Mileage:-   1,312,000
Disposal:- Swindon 24.3.1977

Notable Events:

1965
August worked Ian Allan test special, the outward bound "Cornish Riviera Express".

D1058 picks up the front portion of the train which will form part of its London working on 18th August 1976.

D1058 Western Nobleman *waits the next turn of duty at Exeter stabling point, 18th August 1976.*

D1065 WESTERN CONSORT

BUILT: Crewe 18.6.1963 (DE LOT 286)

LIVERY: 1. On entering service:-
           Maroon with half yellow panel.
        2. Between 1967 and 1971:-
           Rail Blue with full yellow ends.

DEPOT ALLOCATIONS:-
JUN 1963   –   81A OLD OAK COMMON
JAN 1964   –   84A LAIRA
MAR 1969   –   82A BRISTOL BATH ROAD
OCT 1971   –   84A LAIRA

WITHDRAWN:-   4.11.1976
Reason:-   Planned withdrawal
Mileage:-   1,288,000
Disposal:-   Swindon 22.11.1976

D1065 Western Consort arriving at Bodmin Road from Penzance 14th August 1976. Note the shabby condition of these locos as they neared the end of their days.

D1065 at Bodmin Road waiting to draw forward and looking the worse for wear.

D1068 WESTERN RELIANCE

BUILT: Crewe 12.7.1963 (DE LOT 286)

LIVERY: 1. On entering service:-
             Maroon with half yellow warning panels.
         2. From approx. 1968:-
             Maroon with full yellow panels.
         3. Between 1967 and 1971 onwards:-
             Rail Blue with full yellow ends.

DEPOT ALLOCATIONS:-

JULY 1963	–	81A OLD OAK COMMON
JAN 1964	–	84A LAIRA
APR 1964	–	83A NEWTON ABBOT
JUNE 1964	–	82A BRISTOL BATH ROAD
SEPT 1965	–	84A LAIRA
JULY 1969	–	87E LANDORE
APR 1970	–	84A LAIRA
OCT 1970	–	87A LANDORE
OCT 1971	–	84A LAIRA

WITHDRAWN:- 12.10.1976
Reason:-   'B' end final drive seized
Mileage:-   1,312,000
Disposal:-   Swindon 12.10.1976
              Prior to being cut up, this locomotive was used as a disguise for D1062 *Western Courier,* on the turntable within Swindon Works, whilst the latter, which had previously occupied this spot for a considerable time, underwent restoration for the Western Locomotive Association.

Notable Events:

1976

March 5th worked a Newbury Races vintage train special. "Made in Japan" had been chalked under the nameplate! The train included Gresley buffet car No. W9135E which was built c1936. Bookies in trilby hats and loud suits completed the scene which was about as "vintage" as one would see.

D1070 WESTERN GAUNTLET

BUILT: Crewe 28.10.1963 (DE LOT 286)

LIVERY: 1. On entering service:-
             Maroon with half yellow warning panel.
         2. Between 1967 and 1971 onwards:-
             Rail Blue with full yellow ends.

DEPOT ALLOCATIONS:-

OCT 1963	–	86A CARDIFF CANTON
MAR 1964	–	87E LANDORE
APR 1966	–	84A LAIRA
FEB 1969	–	87E LANDORE
MAY 1971	–	84A LAIRA

WITHDRAWN:- 30.12.1976
Reason:-   'B' end collision damage
Mileage:-   1,312,000
Disposal:-   Swindon 24.3.1977

Previous pages:
D1068 Western Reliance *posed a her base depot on a lovely summer morning of 1976.*

D1070 Western Gauntlet *leaving Plymouth North Road bound for Paddington, 13th August 1976.*

D1071 at London Paddington at the head of a return excursion to South Wales, 7th December 1974.
(N. E. Preedy)

D1071 WESTERN RENOWN

BUILT: Crewe 7.11.1963 (DE LOT 286)

LIVERY: 1. On entering service:-
            Maroon with half yellow panels.
          2. Between 1967 and 1971 onwards:-
            Rail Blue with full yellow ends.

DEPOT ALLOCATIONS:-

NOV 1963	–	81A OLD OAK COMMON
APR 1964	–	83A NEWTON ABBOT
JUN 1964	–	82A BRISTOL BATH ROAD
APR 1968	–	87E LANDORE
AUG 1968	–	84A LAIRA
OCT 1969	–	87E LANDORE
MAR 1970	–	84A LAIRA
APR 1970	–	87A LANDORE
JUN 1970	–	84A LAIRA

WITHDRAWN:- 7.12.1976
Reason:-   'B' end final drive and Cardan shaft seized
Mileage:-   1,232,000
Disposal:-   Swindon 23.2.1977

Notable Events:

1967
In January it suffered a serious collision at St. Anne's Park near Bristol whilst at the head of a Paddington-Swansea passenger train, which was travelling at approximately 15 mph. The locomotive collided with the rear of another passenger train which had been halted at signals. The leading cab was a "write off" with the control desk pushed back almost to the bulkhead. Luckily the crew survived the accident, as they had been able to move back into the engine room compartment prior to the impact.

    This locomotive was also chosen, with certain other members of the Western fleet, to be fitted with the square cab ventilation panel which can be clearly seen on the front of the locomotive.

D1071 Western Renown *seen here immaculate at Westbury depot 15th November 1975.*

(N. E. Preedy)

D1072 WESTERN GLORY

BUILT: Crewe 7.11.1963 (DE LOT 286)

LIVERY: 1. On entering service:-
            Maroon with half yellow panels.
          2. Between 1967 and 1971 onwards:-
            Rail Blue with full yellow ends.

DEPOT ALLOCATIONS:-

NOV 1963	–	81A OLD OAK COMMON
JAN 1966	–	84A LAIRA
JUN 1969	–	82A BRISTOL BATH ROAD
OCT 1971	–	84A LAIRA

WITHDRAWN:- 2.11.1976
Reason:-   Planned withdrawal
Mileage:-   1,280,000
Disposal:-   Swindon 26.1.1977

D1072 Western Glory *at Old Oak Common, 25th July 1976.*

Swindon
(November & December 1976)

D1057 Western Chieftain *and* *D1064* Western Regent *await their end, Swindon 7th November 1976.*

D1049 Western Monarch . . . just a
gutted shell at Swindon scrapyard
on the 21st November 1976.

D1016 Western Gladiator *await* the breaker's torch in Swindo Yard, *21st November 1976.*

The remains of D1016 Wester Gladiator *7th November 1976.*

D1012 Western Firebrand *on the Swindon dump, 7th November 1976.*

D1028 Western Hussar *in Swindon Yard November 1976. Note collision damage.*

D1051 Western Ambassador derelict and waiting for the breaker's torch at Swindon.

D1057 Western Chieftain during its last days at Swindon.

Above: No. D1024 *Western Huntsman* draws away from Taunton with an express for the West of England in August 1973.

Below: No. D1058 *Western Nobleman* skirts the well known sea wall at Dawlish on a sunny August day, 1973.

Above: A very grubby No. D1058 keeps company with No. D1010 *Western Campaigner* at Westbury depot on 3rd January 1977.

Left: No. D1016 *Western Gladiator* pilots a 'Peak' class diesel electric with a train from Penzance along the Devon coast at Dawlish, August 1973.

Westerns Preserved

Above: No. D1013 *Western Ranger* in preservation on the Severn Valley Railway 1st June 1980. The livery is a representation of the desert sand style as originally carried by No. D1000.

Below: The beautifully finished No. D1015 *Western Champion* as restored by the Diesel Traction Group. It is seen at Swindon on 22nd September 1985 having been re-painted in its original experimental golden ochre livery with yellow 'T' end.

(C. Guntripp)

D 1041 Western Prince

Above: In a rather run down state with rust much in evidence, D1041 arrives at its base depot of Plymouth Laira, 16th August 1976.

Below: BREL Crewe Works, 4th February 1988. A change of fortune for the *Prince!* Now resplendent in maroon livery, having been restored by BREL under the ownership of Mr. David Edleston. The locomotive was originally out-shopped on 28th August 1962 as the 289th diesel built at this world famous works.

Western Liveries

Liveries adopted for the Westerns, especially in the beginning, were numerous and varied. There were no less than seven basic colours with variations applied to the class during their service with BR.

The terms Coach Maroon and Loco Maroon referred to hereafter, were terms used by BR on official livery diagrams. However, to the author's best knowledge this does not necessarily imply a colour change. One reason for the differentiation in terms may be that coach enamel did not react kindly to diesel oil and that a new 'mix' was concocted for locomotives which was of a much more durable nature. Another theory is that the term Coach Maroon may have been derived from the GW coaching stock and was used as an initial colour reference for some of the early Westerns. Meanwhile, BR held a competition to establish public opinion on the most favoured livery for these locomotives and maroon was the overall winner. Hence, BR may then have adopted the official term Loco Maroon.

During November 1961, trials commenced on D1000 *Western Enterprise,* which was subjected to various insignia modifications before finally being released to traffic on 20th December of that year. It was turned out from Swindon Works in the experimental Desert Sand livery, initially displaying special name and number plates somewhat smaller in size to the unique design which was finally adopted and retained until withdrawal in 1974. These can now be seen in the Swindon Railway Museum. The letters ''A'' and ''B'' displayed below the cab door, which indicate the ''A'' and ''B'' end of the locomotive, were originally of cast aluminium, but were later replaced by black painted letters. The steel grounds surrounding the cab windows were initially grey but later changed to gloss black. The roof hatches between bulkheads were to be seen as grey spec. BSS 2660: 9-101 prior to being darkened as specified later.

D1000 *Western Enterprise* was the first of the class to enter traffic from Swindon Works, and maintained the experimental Desert Sand livery until approximately 1964, but with the addition of yellow warning panels to spec. BSS 2660:0-003 which were applied to both ends in late 1962. The locomotive was repainted maroon with white window frame surrounds but maintaining her chrome emblems until repainting in Rail Blue between 1967–71.

Close on her heels was D1001 *Western Pathfinder,* which was turned out during February 1962. This locomotive was to be seen in the early livery of Coach Maroon with pale yellow buffer beams and stocks. Official evidence suggests that this locomotive might have initially supported grey roof hatches to spec. BSS 2660:9-094. However, at the time of writing there was no photographic evidence to support this, but D1001 was unique in displaying white window frame surrounds at that time.

Other Swindon built locomotives to carry the maroon livery but with black roof hatches and grey window frame surrounds were: Nos D1005 to D1009. This livery being applied between January 1962 and September 1962.

First of the Standard Green liveried locomotives to emerge from Swindon Works was D1002 *Western Explorer.* Turned out during March 1962, it displayed name and number plates with red grounds, half yellow warning panels and red buffer beam and stocks. D1003 *Western Pioneer* and D1004 *Western Crusader* followed.

The first four Crewe built locomotives also supporting green livery, were Nos D1035 to D1038. The livery was applied between March and September 1962. D1036, D1037 and D1004 remained in this livery until 1967 when the final scheme of Rail Blue was adopted for all British Rail locomotives.

First Loco Maroon liveried Crewe built Westerns were: D1039 to D1042. Each supported a deeper shade of yellow buffer beam and stocks than their Swindon counterparts, also the yellow extended over the beading of the buffer beam surround on locomotives D1039 and D1040. On Nos D1041 and D1042 the yellow extended over the recessed area and up to the beading only. These locomotives carried black roof hatches between bulkheads.

D1002 Western Explorer *at Old
Oak Common, 23rd September
1962. Livery is green with yellow
end panels and red buffer beams
and stocks with red name and
numberplate grounds, as Swindon
built examples. (N. Skinner cour-
esy D. H. Edleston).*

Loco Maroon had now become the chosen livery for all the Western
locomotives. This supported the new design of black buffer beam and
stocks and it was applied between 27th September 1962 and 7th March
1967, with the exception of D1015, described later.

D1043 *Western Duke* was the first to receive the new livery when
turned out from Crewe on 26th October 1962, also around this period it
was decided to apply yellow warning panels to both ends of all
locomotives. There was, however, an interim period between the time
the livery was adopted and the application of panels, so certain
locomotives did in fact run completely in Loco Maroon.

As mentioned earlier, D1015 *Western Champion* was an initial
exception. It appeared from Swindon Works on 21st January 1963,
supporting the new experimental livery of Golden Ochre, this being a
precise match to Stroudley's 'improved engine green' and was at the
suggestion of the late Brian Haresnape. Also an experimental "T"
shaped warning panel was applied to one end only, supported by a
modified yellow patch on the other. However it only sported this for a
short while, but did in fact maintain the Golden Ochre until after hauling
the returning empty stock of Winston Churchill's funeral train in 1965.
D1015 was repainted maroon in that year.

The final experimental livery from Swindon Works was to be
Chromatic Blue, applied in the first instance to D1030 *Western
Musketeer* during September 1966. This consisted of red buffer beams
and stocks, yellow warning panels and a small British Rail 'coming-and-
going' emblem. This was to be the forerunner of the now standard Rail
Blue livery with which we are familiar.

D1030 maintained that livery until receiving its final livery of Rail
Blue between 1967 and 1971.

Other locomotives to support an experimental blue livery were
D1017, D1036, D1037, D1043, D1047 and D1057. These were outshopped
with black buffer beams and stocks. As half yellow warning panels were
still in vogue at that time, these locomotives carried them whilst finished
in the experimental livery. The standard Rail Blue livery was adopted by
British Rail for all locomotives and was applied to the Class from 7th
March 1967 onwards.

It was later decided to adopt the full yellow ends for all locomotives,
consequently those which had maintained the maroon livery during this
period received full yellow ends before their final livery of Rail Blue. A
few examples were:

D1001 WESTERN PATHFINDER	D1039 WESTERN KING
D1002 WESTERN EXPLORER	D1041 WESTERN PRINCE
D1007 WESTERN TALISMAN	D1044 WESTERN DUCHESS
D1008 WESTERN HARRIER	D1045 WESTERN VISCOUNT
D1012 WESTERN FIREBRAND	D1046 WESTERN MARQUIS
D1016 WESTERN GLADIATOR	D1056 WESTERN SULTAN
D1025 WESTERN GUARDSMAN	D1061 WESTERN ENVOY
D1031 WESTERN RIFLEMAN	D1067 WESTERN DRUID
D1032 WESTERN MARKSMAN	D1068 WESTERN RELIANCE

Rail Blue livery in itself took various forms of insignia. During the
1967 period from when the livery was first introduced, certain
locomotives still carried the red route availability disc centrally beneath
the number plate at both ends. This was officially deleted on 17th
December 1968 and replaced by the familiar locomotive data panels.

Certain locomotives carried the route availability disc as well as the
loco data panel until the end, the disc simply being re-positioned. Known
examples were: D1001; D1013; D1036 and D1058.

Some of the early blue liveried Westerns were noted as carrying
oval depot code plate stickers to the right hand side of the cab door, as
well as the original cast plates which were mounted on the locomotive
front end skirts. However they were later removed. (See diagram E.G.1
for details).

Another exception to the adopted standard blue livery was that of
D1013 *Western Ranger*. It was adorned with red name and number

1039 Western King *at Old Oak
Common, 23rd September 1962.
Maroon livery with yellow buffer
beams and stocks with the yellow
continuing over the beading, as
with D1040* Western Queen, *the
only other Crewe built 'Western'
to have this feature.*

*N. Skinner courtesy D. H. Edles-
on)*

plates, white wheel rim and silver buffers; perhaps a symbol of its rail tour status given to her by British Rail staff.

Finally, the most widely adopted scheme to be applied by British Rail in later days was to the body area including fixed roof areas, louvres, cab hatches and roof hatches between bulkheads – Rail Blue. Front ends to skirt and window surrounds – yellow. Buffer beams and stocks – black. Battery box catches picked out in yellow. Name and number plate base plate were of mild steel painted gloss black. The beading was of aluminium to spec. N.E. 4 BSS 1476 as British Aluminium Co. Pattern No. DBB10. The letters and numbers were also aluminium to spec. BSS 1490 LM20 and had polished faces. These specs applied to all liveries throughout the life of the locomotive. The depot code plate was later applied symmetrically, directly above the number plate and red LA (Laira) becoming the standard depot for all locomotives. In later days the original cast depot and works plates were removed.

In conclusion, whilst this is a most difficult subject to use pin-point accuracy, and the authenticity cannot be fully guaranteed, the facts set out are intended as a guide to the model maker or preservationist, for whom I hope it will make interesting reading.

D1041 Western Prince *as origi nally turned out from Crewe. Liv ery is maroon with yellow buffe beams and stocks up to th beading only. D1042* Wester Princess *was the only other Crew built Class 52 to be so treated. (A. Noble courtesy D. H. Edlestor.*

Easy Reference Livery Chart

Note:-

a) All locomotives except D1004, D1036 and D1037 irrespective of experimental liveries were designated Loco Maroon with small yellow panels during the period 27th September 1962 to 7th March 1967.

b) All locomotives were painted Rail Blue with full yellow ends from 7th March 1967 onwards.

1	D1000	WESTERN ENTERPRISE	2 & 5	D1037	WESTERN EMPRESS
6	D1001	WESTERN PATHFINDER	2	D1038	WESTERN SOVEREIGN
2	D1002	WESTERN EXPLORER	7	D1039	WESTERN KING
2	D1003	WESTERN KING	7	D1040	WESTERN QUEEN
2	D1004	WESTERN CRUSADER	7	D1041	WESTERN PRINCE
6	D1005	WESTERN VENTURER	7	D1042	WESTERN PRINCESS
6	D1006	WESTERN STALWART	5	D1043	WESTERN DUKE
6	D1007	WESTERN TALISMAN		D1044	WESTERN DUCHESS
6	D1008	WESTERN HARRIER		D1045	WESTERN VISCOUNT
6	D1009	WESTERN INVADER		D1046	WESTERN MARQUIS
	D1010	WESTERN CAMPAIGNER	5	D1047	WESTERN LORD
	D1011	WESTERN THUNDERER		D1048	WESTERN LADY
	D1012	WESTERN FIREBRAND		D1049	WESTERN MONARCH
	D1013	WESTERN RANGER		D1050	WESTERN RULER
	D1014	WESTERN LEVIATHAN		D1051	WESTERN AMBASSADOR
3	D1015	WESTERN CHAMPION		D1052	WESTERN VICEROY
	D1016	WESTERN GLADIATOR		D1053	WESTERN PATRIARCH
5	D1017	WESTERN WARRIOR		D1054	WESTERN GOVERNOR
	D1018	WESTERN BUCCANEER		D1055	WESTERN ADVOCATE
	D1019	WESTERN CHALLENGER		D1056	WESTERN SULTAN
	D1020	WESTERN HERO	5	D1057	WESTERN CHIEFTAN
	D1021	WESTERN CAVALIER		D1058	WESTERN NOBLEMAN
	D1022	WESTERN SENTINEL		D1059	WESTERN EMPIRE
	D1023	WESTERN FUSILIER		D1060	WESTERN DOMINION
	D1024	WESTERN HUNTSMAN		D1061	WESTERN ENVOY
	D1025	WESTERN GUARDSMAN		D1062	WESTERN COURIER
	D1026	WESTERN CENTURION		D1063	WESTERN MONITOR
	D1027	WESTERN LANCER		D1064	WESTERN REGENT
	D1028	WESTERN HUSSAR		D1065	WESTERN CONSORT
	D1029	WESTERN LEGIONNAIRE		D1066	WESTERN PREFECT
4	D1030	WESTERN MUSKETEER		D1067	WESTERN DRUID
	D1031	WESTERN RIFLEMAN		D1068	WESTERN RELIANCE
	D1032	WESTERN MARKSMAN		D1069	WESTERN VANGUARD
	D1033	WESTERN TROOPER		D1070	WESTERN GAUNTLET
	D1034	WESTERN DRAGOON		D1071	WESTERN RENOWN
2	D1035	WESTERN YEOMAN		D1072	WESTERN GLORY
2 & 5	D1036	WESTERN EMPEROR		D1073	WESTERN BULWARK

1. **DESERT SAND** – Experimental livery – designated Nov. 1961 to Sept. 1962.
2. **STANDARD GREEN** – With small yellow panels designated March 1962 to Sept. 1962.
3. **GOLDEN OCHRE** – With special panels applied 1963.
4. **CHROMATIC BLUE** – Experimental livery applied 1966 (with red buffer beams and stocks).
5. **CHROMATIC BLUE VARIATION** – With black buffer beams and stocks applied 1966.
6. **COACH MAROON** – Designated to Swindon built locos within period Jan. 1st 1962 to Sept. 27th 1962 (Yellow buffer beams and stocks).
7. **COACH/LOCO MAROON** – As above but to Crewe built locos with darker yellow buffer beams carried up to and over beading.

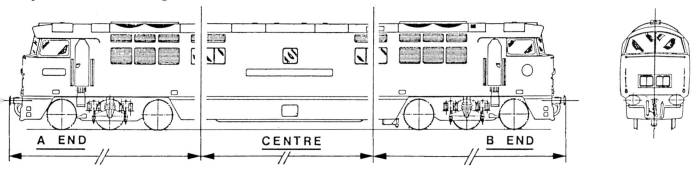

A END   CENTRE   B END

KEY TO LIVERY DIAGRAMS

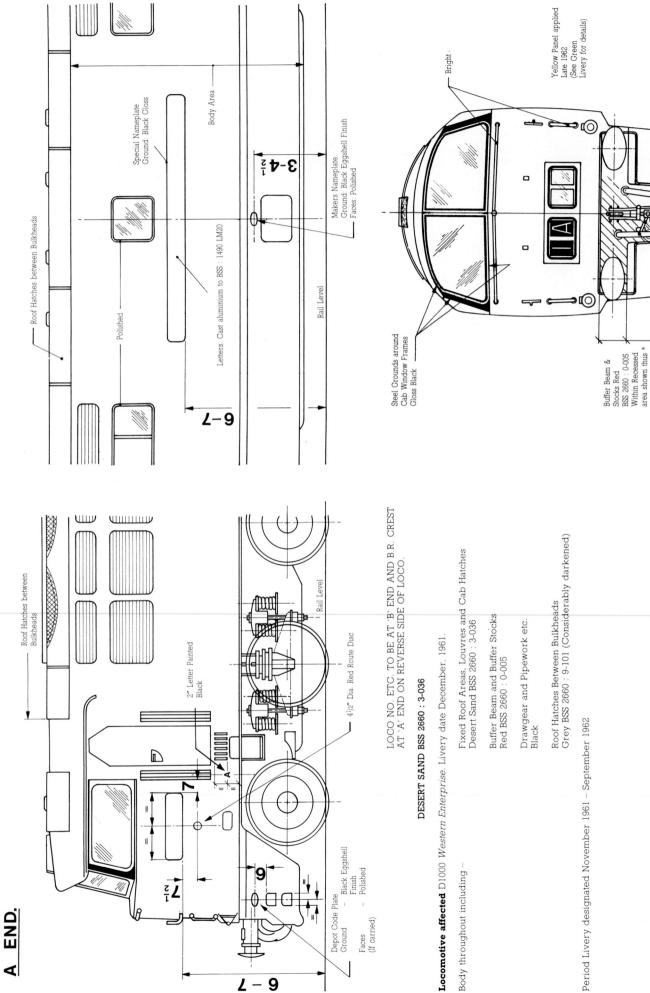

A END.

Roof Hatches between Bulkheads

Roof Hatches between Bulkheads

2" Letter Painted Black

4½" Dia. Red Route Disc

Polished

Depot Code Plate
Ground – Black Eggshell Finish
Faces – Polished
(If carried)

Special Nameplate
Ground Black Gloss

Body Area

Makers Nameplate
Ground Black Eggshell Finish
Faces Polished

Letters Cast aluminium to BSS .1490 LM20

Rail Level

Rail Level

Bright

Yellow Panel applied
Late 1962
(See Green
Livery for details)

Steel Grounds around
Cab Window Frames
Gloss Black

Buffer Beam &
Stocks Red
BSS 2660 : 0-005
Within Recessed
area shown thus *

Drawgear and Pipework etc.

LOCO NO. ETC. TO BE AT 'B' END AND B.R. CREST
AT 'A' END ON REVERSE SIDE OF LOCO.

DESERT SAND BSS 2660 : 3-036

Locomotive affected D1000 *Western Enterprise.* Livery date December, 1961.

Body throughout including –

Fixed Roof Areas, Louvres and Cab Hatches
Desert Sand BSS 2660 : 3-036

Buffer Beam and Buffer Stocks
Red BSS 2660 : 0-005

Drawgear and Pipework etc.
Black

Roof Hatches Between Bulkheads
Grey BSS 2660 : 9-101 (Considerably darkened)

Period Livery designated November 1961 – September 1962

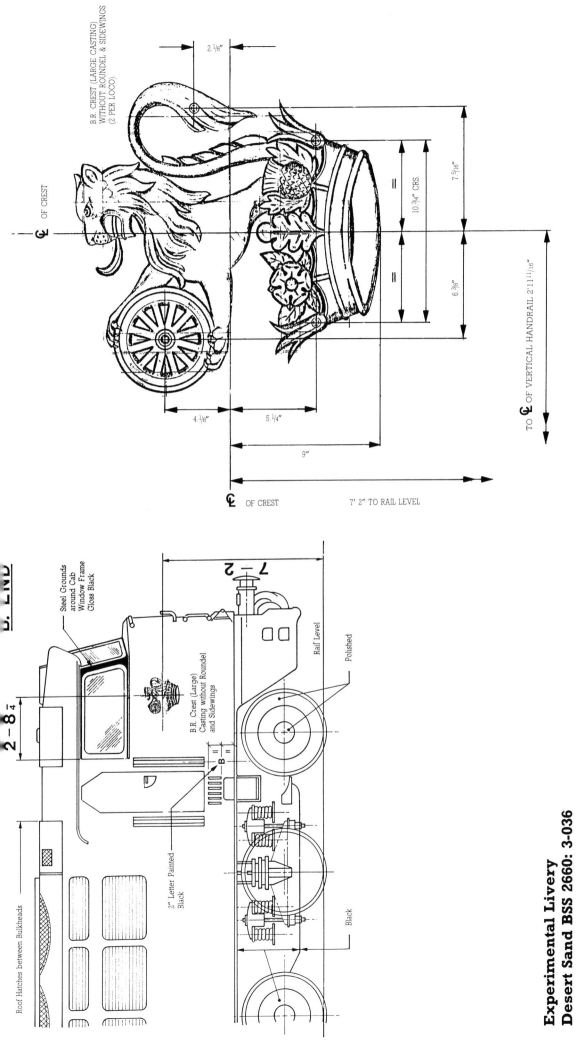

B.R. CREST (LARGE CASTING)
WITHOUT ROUNDEL & SIDEWINGS
(2 PER LOCO).

2.1/8"

₵ OF CREST

7.5/16"

10.3/4" CRS.

6.3/8"

4.1/8"

5.1/4"

9"

TO ₵ OF VERTICAL HANDRAIL 2'11¹¹/₁₆"

₵ OF CREST

7' 2" TO RAIL LEVEL

**B.R. CREST AS APPLIED TO LOCOMOTIVE
D1000 – WESTERN ENTERPRISE
LATE 1961**

B. END

Roof Hatches between Bulkheads

Steel Grounds
around Cab
Window Frame
Gloss Black

B.R. Crest (Large)
Casting without Roundel
and Sidewings

2" Letter Painted
Black

2 – 8 ¼

7 – 2

Rail Level

Polished

Black

B

**Experimental Livery
Desert Sand BSS 2660: 3-036**

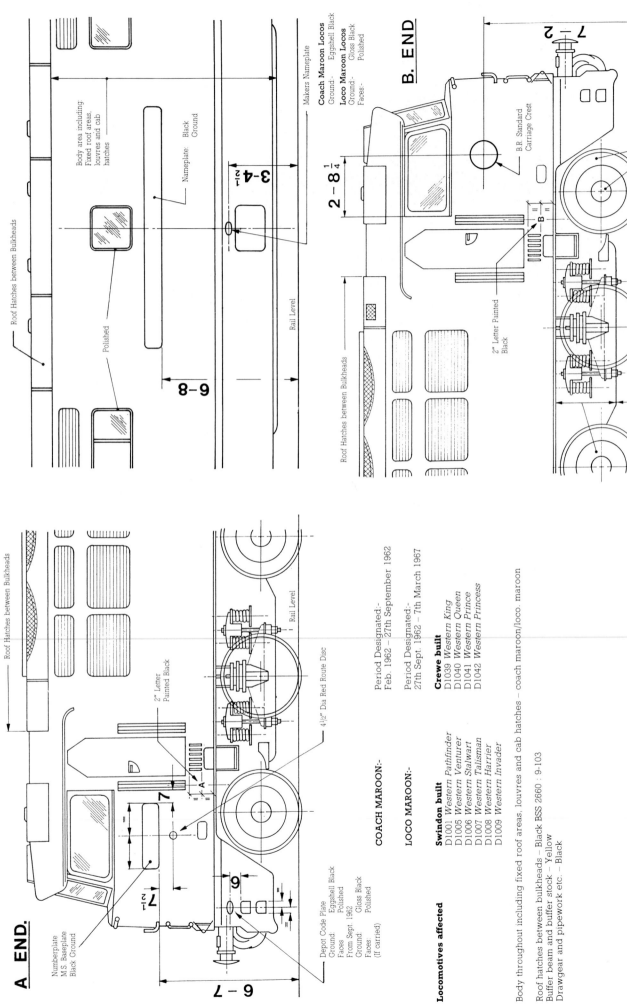

A END.

Numberplate
M S Baseplate
Black Ground

6 - 7

2" Letter
Painted Black

7

9

2½"

7½"

Roof Hatches between Bulkheads

Rail Level

4½" Dia Red Route Disc

Depot Code Plate
Ground   Eggshell Black
Faces   Polished
From Sept. 1962
Ground   Gloss Black
Faces   Polished
(If carried)

COACH MAROON:-

LOCO MAROON:-

Period Designated:-
Feb. 1962 – 27th September 1962

Period Designated:-
27th Sept. 1962 – 7th March 1967

Locomotives affected

Swindon built
D1001 *Western Pathfinder*
D1005 *Western Venturer*
D1006 *Western Stalwart*
D1007 *Western Talisman*
D1008 *Western Harrier*
D1009 *Western Invader*

Crewe built
D1039 *Western King*
D1040 *Western Queen*
D1041 *Western Prince*
D1042 *Western Princess*

Body throughout including fixed roof areas, louvres and cab hatches – coach maroon/loco. maroon

Roof hatches between bulkheads – Black BSS 2660 : 9-103
Buffer beam and buffer stock – Yellow
Drawgear and pipework etc. – Black

Roof Hatches between Bulkheads

Body area including
Fixed roof areas,
louvres and cab
hatches

Nameplate: Black
             Ground

Polished

8 - 9

3 - 4½"

Rail Level

Makers Nameplate

Coach Maroon Locos
Ground:-   Eggshell Black
Loco Maroon Locos
Ground:-   Gloss Black
Faces:-   Polished

B. END

7 - 2

2 - 8¼"

B R Standard
Carriage Crest

2" Letter Painted
Black

Polished

Black

Rail Level

Roof Hatches between Bulkheads

B

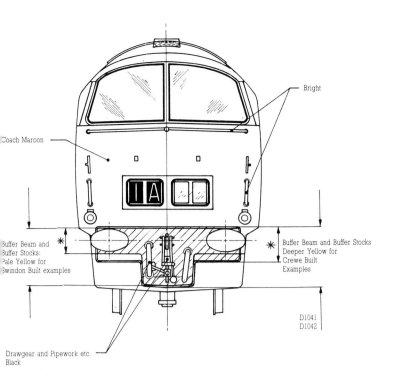

Bright

Coach Maroon

Buffer Beam and Buffer Stocks: Pale Yellow for Swindon Built examples

Buffer Beam and Buffer Stocks Deeper Yellow for Crewe Built Examples

D1041
D1042

Drawgear and Pipework etc. Black

COACH MAROON/LOCO. MAROON

Locomotives affected:

Swindon Built	Crewe Built
D1001 *Western Pathfinder*	D1039 *Western King*
D1005 *Western Venturer*	D1040 *Western Queen*
D1006 *Western Stalwart*	D1041 *Western Prince*
D1007 *Western Talisman*	D1042 *Western Princess*
D1008 *Western Harrier*	
D1009 *Western Invader*	

Note: Swindon built locos had pale yellow buffer beams and stocks up to the beading, within recessed area marked thus*. Crewe built locos had deeper yellow buffer beams and stocks outside the recessed area and over the beading in the case of D1039 and D1040, and up to the beading on D1041 and D1042, as shown.

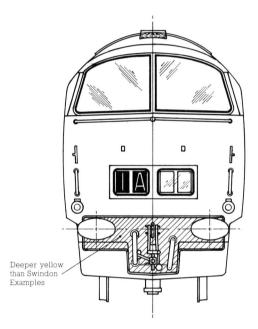

Deeper yellow than Swindon Examples

COACH MAROON/LOCO MAROON CREWE BUILT

D1039 and D1040 *over* recessed area *and* beading.
D1041 and D1042 *over* recessed area but *up to* the beading only

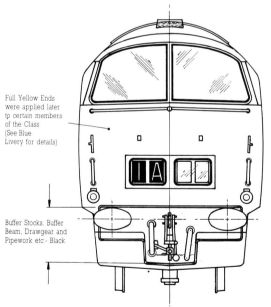

Full Yellow Ends were applied later to certain members of the Class (See Blue Livery for details)

Yellow Panel applied from Sept. 1962 (See Standard Locomotive Green for Details)

Buffer Stocks, Buffer Beam, Drawgear and Pipework etc- Black

LOCO. MAROON

Period:- September 27th 1962 to March 7th 1967

Locomotives affected:-   D1000– D1073
Except D1004, D1036, & D1037

Body throughout including fixed roof areas, louvres and cab hatches – Loco. Maroon.

Roof hatches between Bulkheads – Black BSS 2660 : 9-103

Buffer Beam and Buffer Stocks:- Black
Drawgear and Pipework etc:- Black

A END.

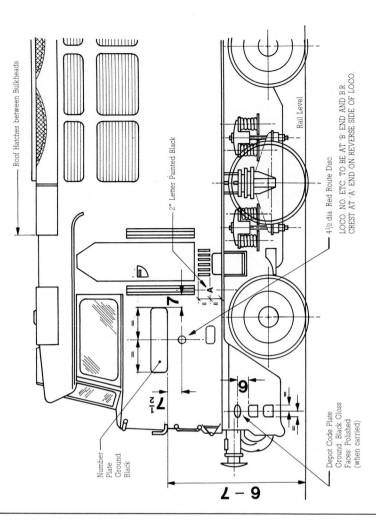

Roof Hatches between Bulkheads

2" Letter Painted Black

4½ dia. Red Route Disc.

LOCO. NO. ETC. TO BE AT B END AND B.R.
CREST AT 'A' END ON REVERSE SIDE OF LOCO

Rail Level

Number Plate Ground Black

Depot Code Plate
Ground. Black Gloss
Faces Polished
(when carried)

Locomotive affected: D1015 *Western Champion*

Body throughout including — Fixed Roof Areas, Louvres and Cab
Hatches: Golden Ochre
Buffer Beam: Golden Ochre
Stocks: Black
Drawgear and Pipework etc: Black
Roof Hatches between Bulkheads: Black

Period Livery applied 1963-1965 with variations.

The livery depicted was as initially turned out from Swindon Works in January 1963. At her time of repainting maroon in 1965, the locomotive was to be seen completely in Golden Ochre livery.

Golden Ochre

A END.

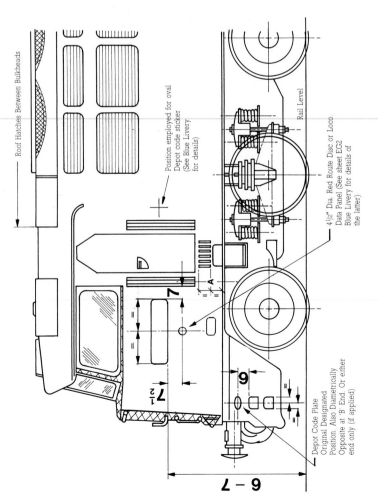

Roof Hatches Between Bulkheads

Position employed for oval
Depot code sticker
(See Blue Livery
for details)

4½" Dia. Red Route Disc or Loco.
Data Panel (See sheet EG2
Blue Livery for details of
the latter)

Rail Level

Depot Code Plate
Original Designated
Position. Also Diametrically
Opposite at 'B' End. Or either
end only (if applied)

MAROON LIVERY INSIGNIA VARIATIONS APPLIED TO
LOCOMOTIVES WITH HALF AND FULL YELLOW WARNING PANELS
AND EXPERIMENTAL BLUE LIVERY

Locomotives affected:- Few examples.

1. Maroon with full yellow ends.   Maroon with half yellow panels.

D1007 *Western Talisman*   D1042 *Western Princess*
D1012 *Western Firebrand*   D1027 *Western Lancer**
D1039 *Western King*
D1045 *Western Viscount**   Experimental Blue Liveries
D1057 *Western Chieftain*
D1037 *Western Empress**
D1030 *Western Musketeer**
(As drawn with depot code plate on the front end skirt.)

Note:
1. Depot code plate on front end skirt deleted unless otherwise stated.
2. All examples listed carried the loco data panel and depot code sticker type 1 unless otherwise stated.
3. Examples marked thus * carried the 4½" dia. red route disc and not data panels at that time.

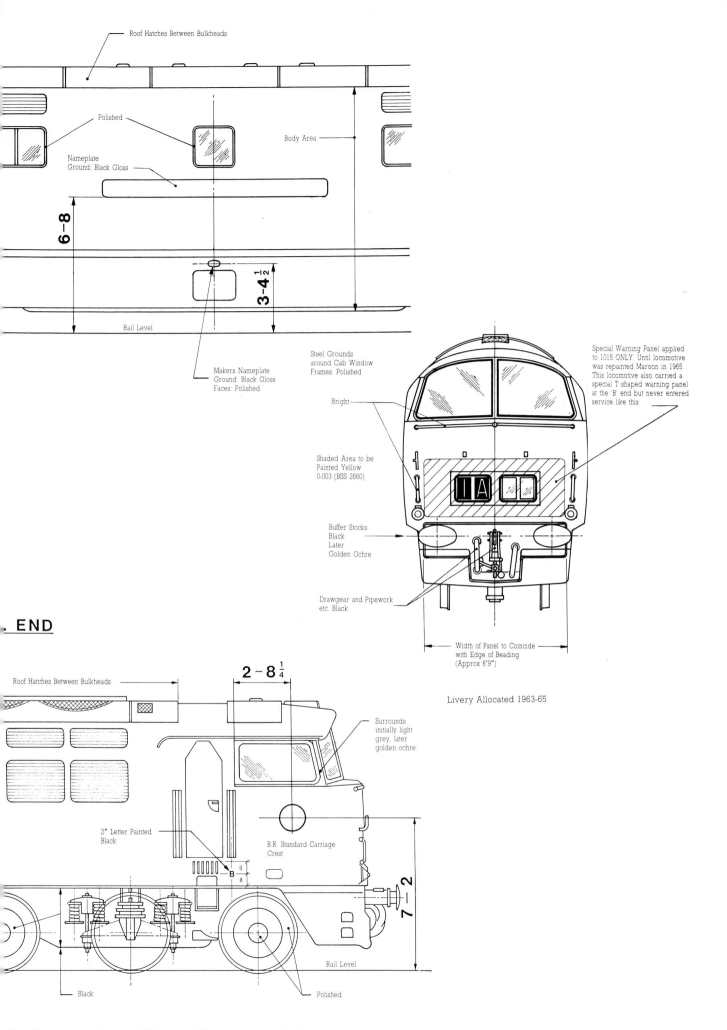

Roof Hatches Between Bulkheads

Polished

Nameplate
Ground: Black Gloss

Body Area

6-8

3-4½

Rail Level

Makers Nameplate
Ground: Black Gloss
Faces: Polished

Steel Grounds
around Cab Window
Frames: Polished

Bright

Special Warning Panel applied
to 1015 ONLY. Until locomotive
was repainted Maroon in 1965.
This locomotive also carried a
special T shaped warning panel
at the 'B' end but never entered
service like this

Shaded Area to be
Painted Yellow
0-003 (BSS 2660)

Buffer Stocks
Black
Later
Golden Ochre

1 A

Drawgear and Pipework
etc. Black

Width of Panel to Coincide
with Edge of Beading
(Approx 6'9")

Livery Allocated 1963-65

. END

Roof Hatches Between Bulkheads

2 - 8¼

Surrounds
initially light
grey, later
golden ochre

2" Letter Painted
Black

B

B.R. Standard Carriage
Crest

7 - 2

Rail Level

Black

Polished

Loco No. etc. to be at 'B' end and B.R. Crest at 'A' end on reverse side of
Loco.

Golden Ochre

A END.

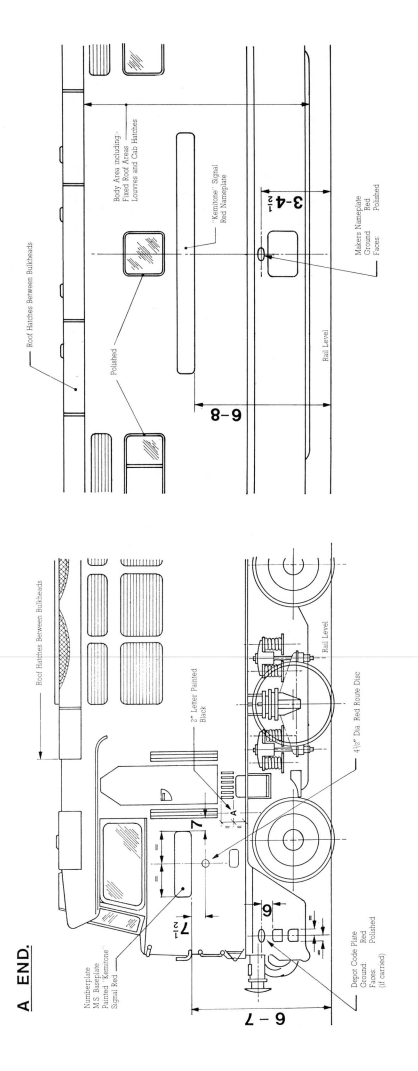

Roof Hatches Between Bulkheads

Body Area including:-
Fixed Roof Areas
Louvres and Cab Hatches

Polished

"Kemitone" Signal
Red Nameplate

Makers Nameplate
Ground   Red
Faces   Polished

3-4 ½

Rail Level

6-8

Roof Hatches Between Bulkheads

Numberplate
M.S. Baseplate
Painted "Kemitone"
Signal Red

2" Letter Painted
Black

7

7 ½

Rail Level

4½" Dia. Red Route Disc

6

Depot Code Plate
Ground   Red
Faces   Polished
(if carried)

6-7

STANDARD LOCOMOTIVE GREEN B.R. SPEC. 30

D1002   *Western Explorer*
D1035   *Western Yeoman*
D1038   *Western Sovereign*

D1003   *Western Pioneer*
D1036   *Western Emperor*

D1004   *Western Crusader*
D1037   *Western Empress*

Body throughout including:

Fixed Roof Areas Louvres and Cab Hatches:
Standard Locomotive Green B.R. Spec. 30
Roof Hatches between Bulkheads:
Mid grey BSS 2660: 9-097
Buffer Beam and Buffer Stocks:
Red BSS 2660 : 0-005
Drawgear and Pipework etc:
Black

Period Livery Designated

March 1962 – September 1962
Except D1004, D1036 and D1037 which remained in
Green until the Rail Blue Livery was applied in 1967.

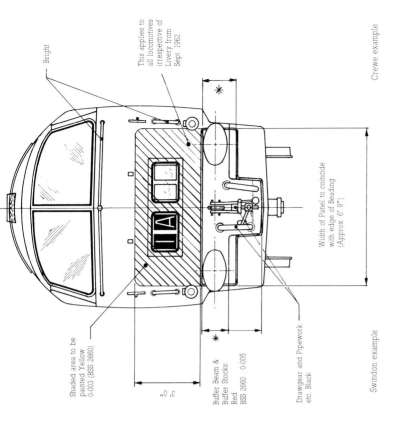

Bright

This applies to all locomotives irrespective of Livery from Sept. 1962

Shaded area to be painted Yellow 0·003 (BSS 2660)

Crewe example

Width of Panel to coincide with edge of Beading (Approx 6' 9")

Buffer Beam & Buffer Stocks Red BSS 2660 0·005

Drawgear and Pipework etc. Black

Swindon example

3' 0"

Date Livery Allocated 1962

Note: Swindon Built Locos had red buffer beams within recessed area marked thus *

Crewe Built Locos had red buffer beams outside recessed area up to beading also shown thus *

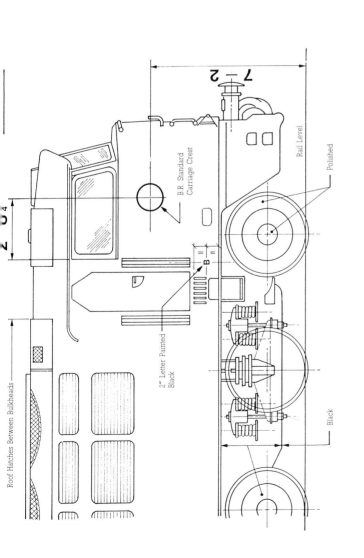

Roof Hatches Between Bulkheads

B.R. Standard Carriage Crest

2" Letter Painted Black

Locomotive number etc. to be at "B" end and B.R. Crest at "A" end on reverse side of locomotive

Rail Level

Polished

Black

7 – 2

2 0 4

B

Standard Locomotive Green B.R. Spec. 30

A END.

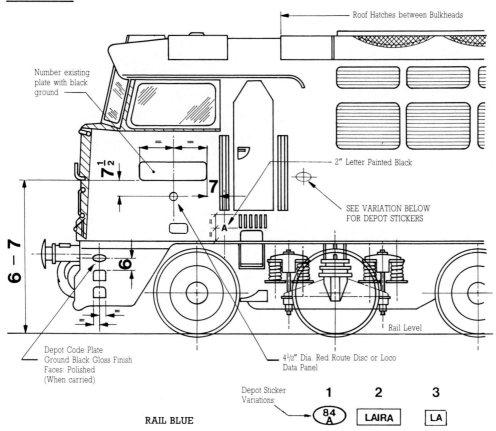

Roof Hatches between Bulkheads

Number existing plate with black ground

$7\frac{1}{2}$

7

6 – 7

6

2" Letter Painted Black

SEE VARIATION BELOW FOR DEPOT STICKERS

A

Rail Level

Depot Code Plate Ground Black Gloss Finish Faces: Polished (When carried)

$4\frac{1}{2}$" Dia. Red Route Disc or Loco Data Panel

Depot Sticker Variations:

1	2	3
84 A	LAIRA	LA

RAIL BLUE

Locomotives affected: D1000-D1073

Body throughout including:
Roof Hatches between Bulkheads:
B. R. Rail Blue
Buffer Stocks, Buffer Beam, Drawgear and pipework etc:
Black
Yellow Warning Colour: BS 0-003 Shown Thus /////

The insignia depicted was applied to maroon, experimental blue and early rail blue liveried locomotives. A few examples of the latter were as follows:-

D1000	*Western Enterprise**†	D1036	*Western Emperor+*
D1006	*Western Stalwart**	D1045	*Western Viscount+*
D1010	*Western Campaigner*	D1053	*Western Patriarch*†*
D1024	*Western Hunstman*	D1060	*Western Dominion*
D1030	*Western Musketeer+*	D1062	*Western Courier*
D1034	*Western Dragoon*	D1073	*Western Bulwark*

Note:
1 Examples listed carried the loco data panel in lieu of the red route disc and ref 1 type depot sticker positioned as shown unless otherwise stated.
2 + Indicates examples carrying a ref. 2 type depot sticker.
3 † Indicates examples fitted with a cast front end skirt shed plate as well as ref. 1 type sticker as depicted above.
4 * Indicates locomotives carried red route disc in lieu of data panel.
5 All the above examples were at this period minus front end skirt depot plates unless indicated otherwise
6 The insignia depicted throughout these livery diagrams is based on photographic evidence of either A or B end only.

Rail Blue

A END.

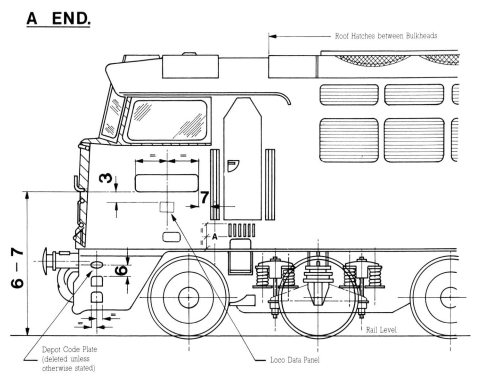

Roof Hatches between Bulkheads

3

7

6 — 7

A

Rail Level

Depot Code Plate
(deleted unless
otherwise stated)

Loco Data Panel

Rail Blue

The following are a few known examples to carry the above insignia
variation.

D1003 *Western Pioneer*   D1053 *Western Patriarch*
D1018 *Western Buccaneer*   D1056 *Western Sultan*
D1048 *Western Lady*   D1072 *Western Glory*
D1051 *Western Ambassador*

A END.

Roof Hatches between Bulkheads

3

7

6 — 7

A

Rail Level

Loco Data Panel

Rail Blue

The above depicted insignia was the final form adopted to the Western
fleet.

It can be assumed that most of the remaining fleet carried this form
from 1974 onwards.

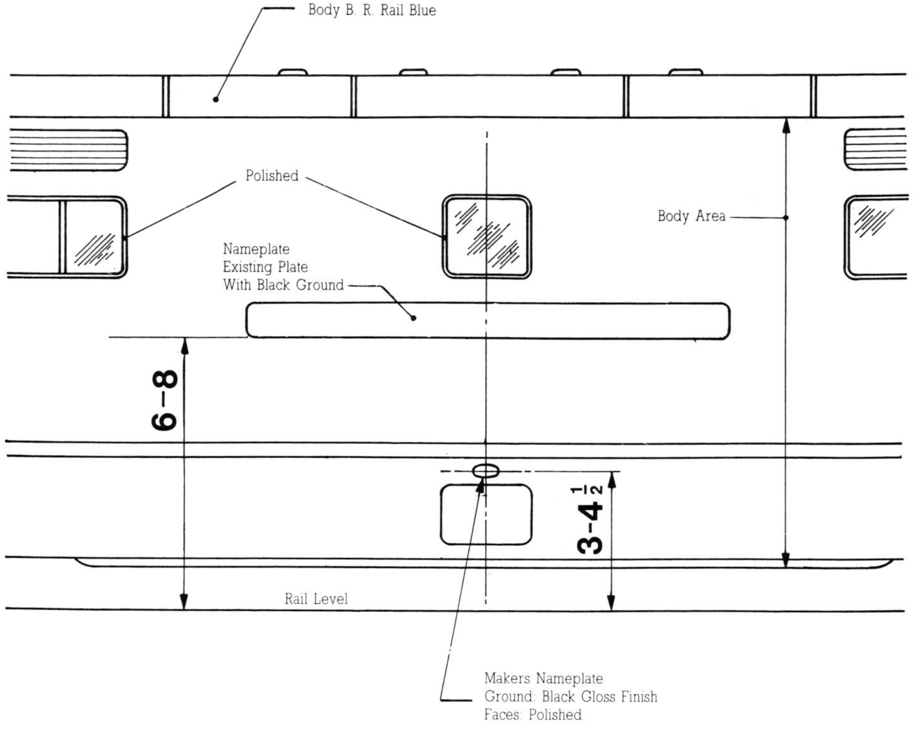

B. R. Symbol 2'6" to be White

Yellow Warning Colour BS 0-003

Roof Hatches between Bulkheads

B. R. Symbol on C/L of Nameplate

2" Letter Painted Black

12

Rail Level

Polished

Black

7 - 2

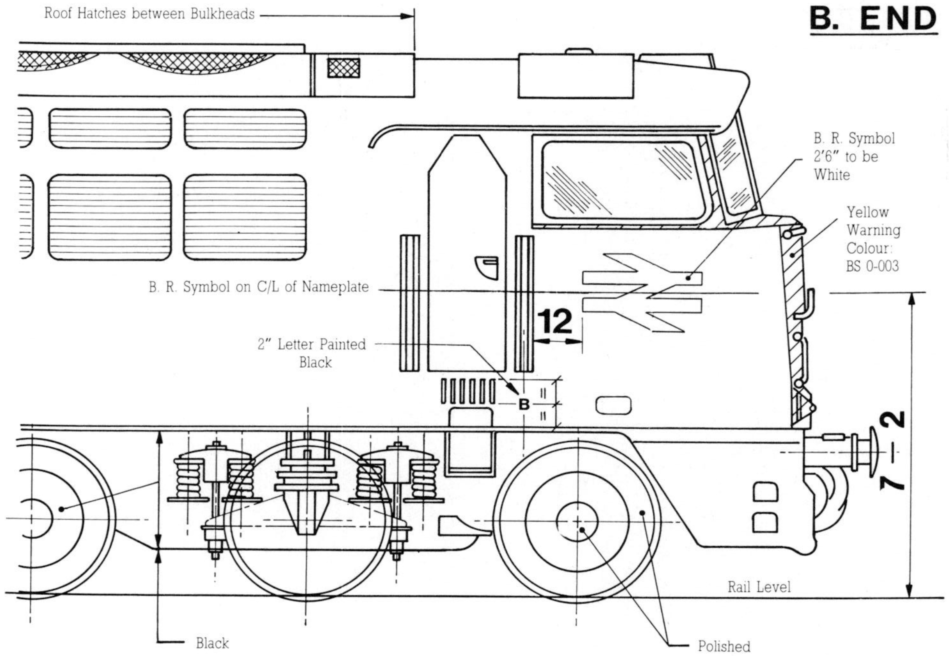

Locomotive No. etc to be at "B" end and B.R. Symbol at "A" end on reverse side of locomotive.

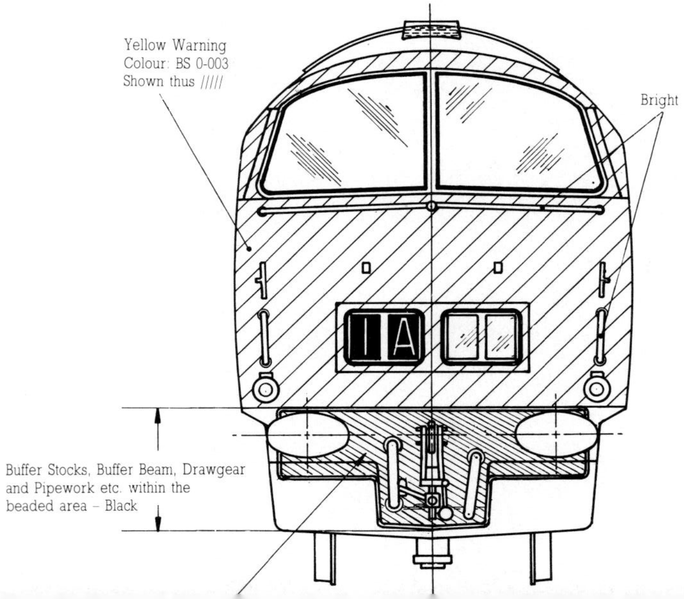

Bright

Yellow Warning Colour BS 0-003 Shown thus /////

Buffer Stocks, Buffer Beam, Drawgear and Pipework etc. within the beaded area - Black

Body B. R. Rail Blue

Polished

Nameplate Existing Plate With Black Ground

Body Area

Makers Nameplate Ground: Black Gloss Finish Faces Polished

3-4 ½

Rail Level

8-9

Rail Blue

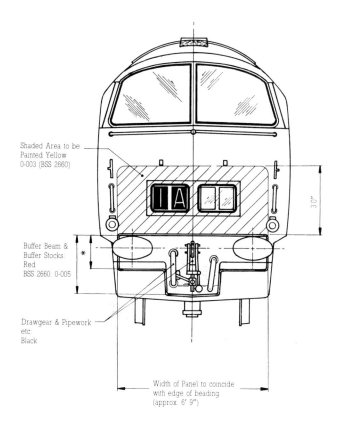

Shaded Area to be
Painted Yellow
0-003 (BSS 2660)

30"

Buffer Beam &
Buffer Stocks:
Red
BSS 2660: 0-005

*

Drawgear & Pipework
etc:
Black

Width of Panel to coincide
with edge of beading
(approx. 6' 9")

Crewe built D1030 *Western Musketeer*

1. * Indicates red is applied over the recessed area.(Crewe style up to beading.)
2. This area was painted black for locomotives D1017, D1036, D1037, D1043, D1047 and D1057

Locomotives affected: D1030 *Western Musketeer*
Body throughout including fixed roof areas,
louvres and cab hatches:
Chromatic Blue
Applied 1966

D1017, D1036, D1037, D1043, D1047 and D1057
Body throughout:-
Chromatic Blue Variants
Buffer Stocks, Buffer Beam, Drawgear and Pipe-
work etc:
Black

It is interesting to note that although this locomotive was first to support the Swindon experimental livery, the buffer beam pattern normally employed on Crewe built and liveried locomotives has been followed.

Experimental Livery
Chromatic Blue

Publisher's note. The livery drawings, pages 126–137, have been prepared from information supplied by the author.

D1002 Western Explorer, *in Standard Locomotive Green with yellow warning panel, heads an 07.30 Shrewsbury to Paddington train. (British Rail)*

D1072 Western Glory *showing the locomotive data panel below the numberplate and depot allocation (LA, Laira) above. Photographed at Old Oak Common, 25th July 1976.*

D1058 Western Nobleman *at Old Oak Common, 8th August 1986, showing cabside detail.*

D1041 Western Prince *as restored at Crewe February 1988, showing footstep details. (See drawing on page 160 for details of pipes and cables.)*

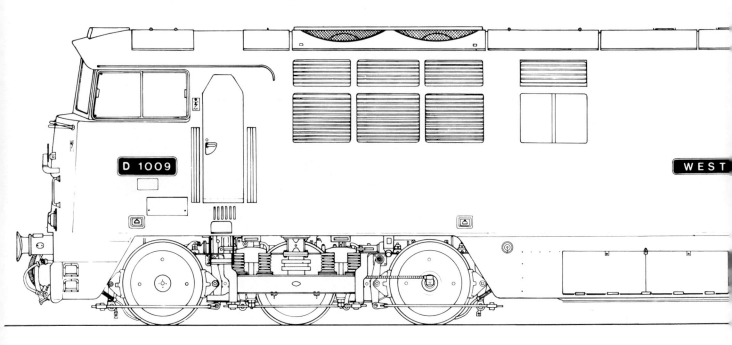

D 1009

WEST

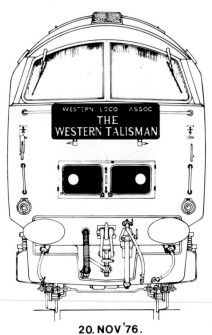

WESTERN LOCO ASSOC
THE
WESTERN TALISMAN

20. NOV '76.

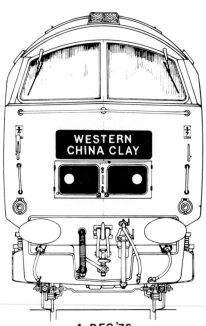

WESTERN
CHINA CLAY

4. DEC. '76.

WESTERN
MEMORIAL

29. JAN. 77.

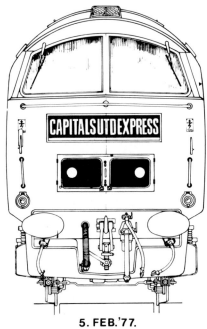

CAPITALSUTDEXPRESS

5. FEB. '77.

Scale: 6 mm = 1 ft.

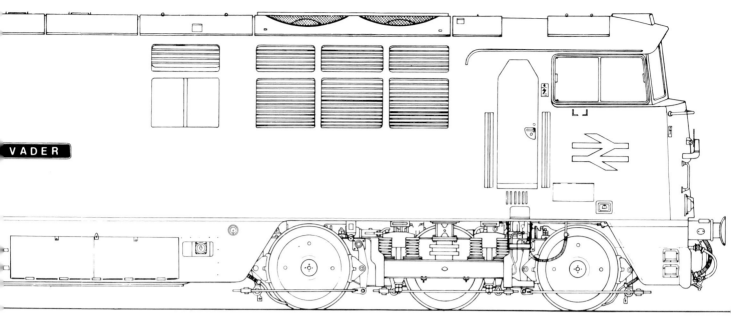

VADER

12. FEB. '77.

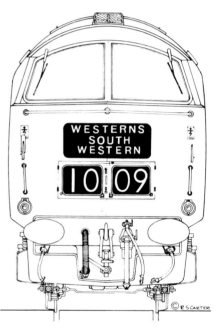

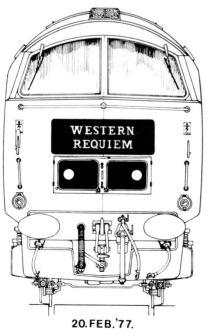

© R.S. Carter

20. FEB. '77.

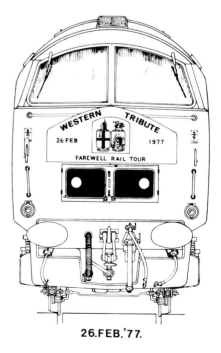

26. FEB. '77.

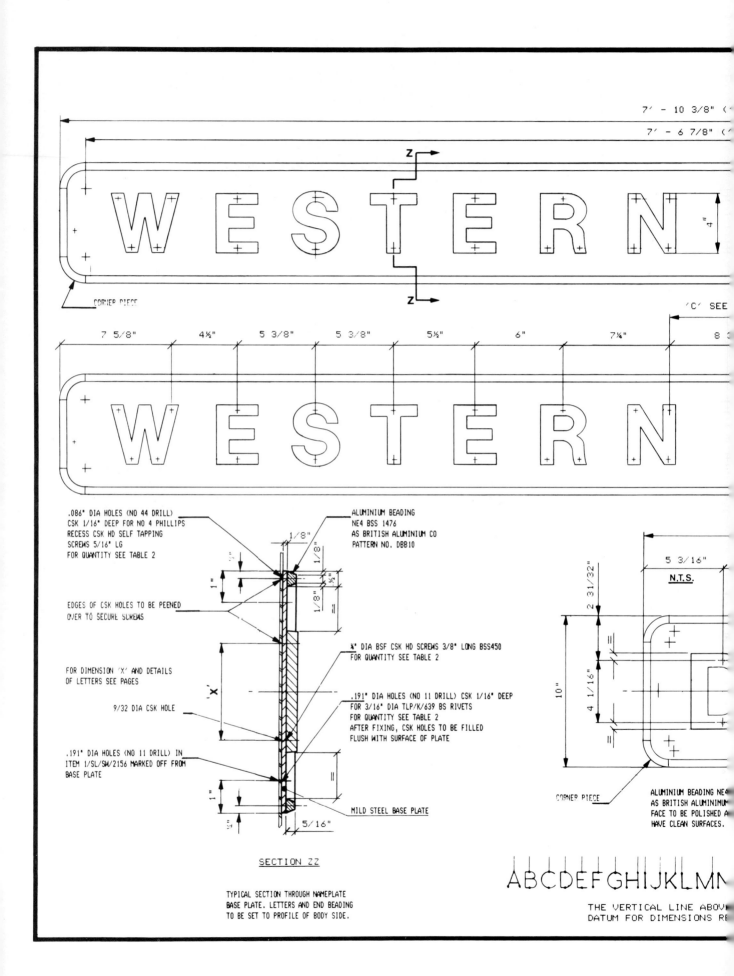

7' - 10 3/8" (1

7' - 6 7/8" (1

Z

Z

CORNER PIECE

'C' SEE

7 5/8"   4½"   5 3/8"   5 3/8"   5½"   6"   7¼"   8 3

.086" DIA HOLES (NO 44 DRILL)
CSK 1/16" DEEP FOR NO 4 PHILLIPS
RECESS CSK HD SELF TAPPING
SCREWS 5/16" LG
FOR QUANTITY SEE TABLE 2

EDGES OF CSK HOLES TO BE PEENED
OVER TO SECURE SCREWS

FOR DIMENSION 'X' AND DETAILS
OF LETTERS SEE PAGES

9/32 DIA CSK HOLE

.191" DIA HOLES (NO 11 DRILL) IN
ITEM 1/SL/SW/2156 MARKED OFF FROM
BASE PLATE

ALUMINIUM BEADING
NE4 BSS 1476
AS BRITISH ALUMINIUM CO
PATTERN NO. DBB10

1/8"
1/8"

1"

1/8"

'X'

X" DIA BSF CSK HD SCREWS 3/8" LONG BSS450
FOR QUANTITY SEE TABLE 2

.191" DIA HOLES (NO 11 DRILL) CSK 1/16" DEEP
FOR 3/16" DIA TLP/K/639 BS RIVETS
FOR QUANTITY SEE TABLE 2
AFTER FIXING, CSK HOLES TO BE FILLED
FLUSH WITH SURFACE OF PLATE

1"

5/16"

MILD STEEL BASE PLATE

SECTION ZZ

TYPICAL SECTION THROUGH NAMEPLATE
BASE PLATE, LETTERS AND END BEADING
TO BE SET TO PROFILE OF BODY SIDE.

5 3/16"

N.T.S.

2 31/32"

10"

4 1/16"

CORNER PIECE

ALUMINIUM BEADING NE4
AS BRITISH ALUMINIUM
FACE TO BE POLISHED A
HAVE CLEAN SURFACES.

ABCDEFGHIJKLMN

THE VERTICAL LINE ABOV
DATUM FOR DIMENSIONS RE

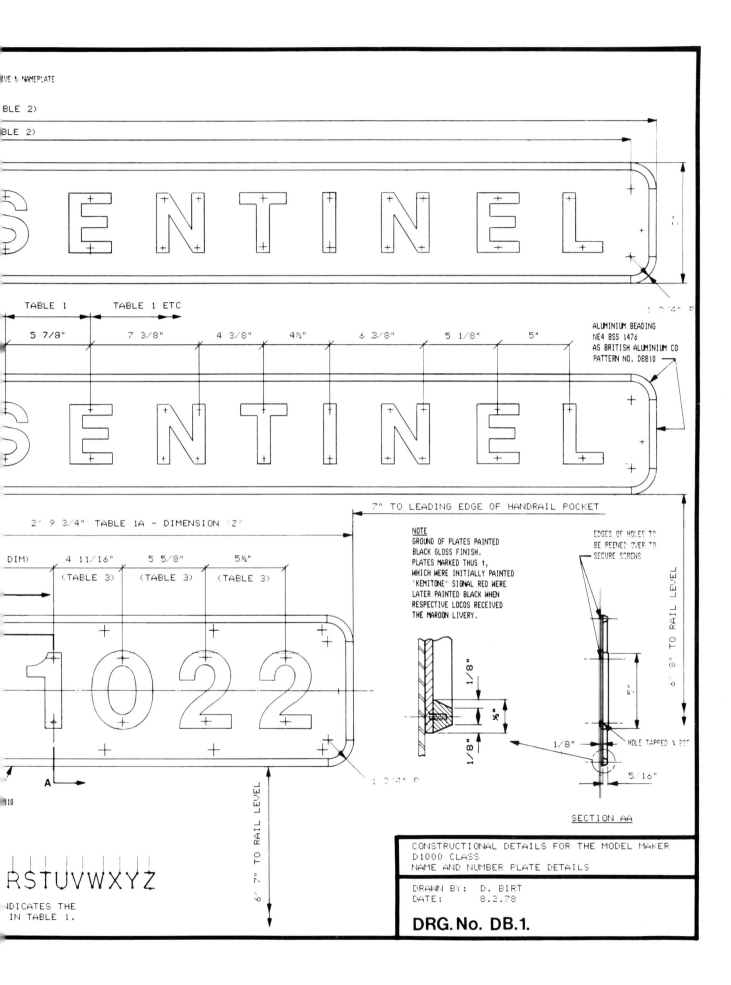

IVE & NAMEPLATE

BLE 2)

BLE 2)

SENTINEL

TABLE 1 | TABLE 1 ETC

5 7/8" | 7 3/8" | 4 3/8" | 4½" | 6 3/8" | 5 1/8" | 5"

ALUMINIUM BEADING
NE4 BSS 1476
AS BRITISH ALUMINIUM CO
PATTERN NO. DBB10

SENTINEL

1 3/4" R

2' 9 3/4" TABLE 1A – DIMENSION 'Z'

7" TO LEADING EDGE OF HANDRAIL POCKET

DIM) | 4 11/16" | 5 5/8" | 5¼"

(TABLE 3) | (TABLE 3) | (TABLE 3)

NOTE
GROUND OF PLATES PAINTED
BLACK GLOSS FINISH.
PLATES MARKED THUS †,
WHICH WERE INITIALLY PAINTED
'KEMITONE' SIGNAL RED WERE
LATER PAINTED BLACK WHEN
RESPECTIVE LOCOS RECEIVED
THE MAROON LIVERY.

EDGES OF HOLES TO
BE PEENED OVER TO
SECURE SCREWS

1022

A

810

SECTION AA

RSTUVWXYZ

NDICATES THE
IN TABLE 1.

CONSTRUCTIONAL DETAILS FOR THE MODEL MAKER
D1000 CLASS
NAME AND NUMBER PLATE DETAILS

DRAWN BY: D. BIRT
DATE: 8.2.78

DRG. No. DB.1.

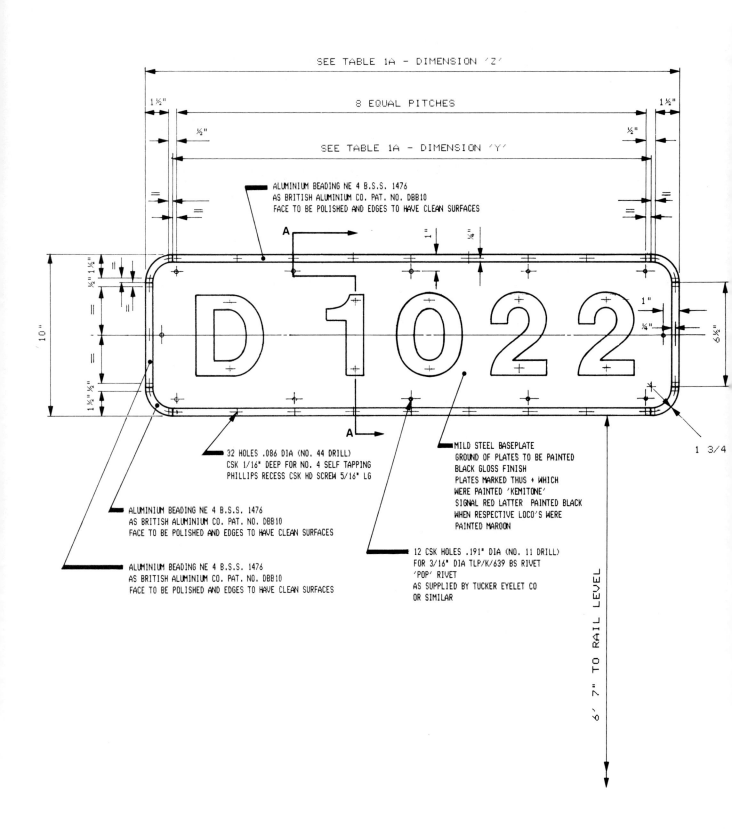

SEE TABLE 1A — DIMENSION 'Z'

1½" 8 EQUAL PITCHES 1½"

½" SEE TABLE 1A — DIMENSION 'Y' ½"

ALUMINIUM BEADING NE 4 B.S.S. 1476
AS BRITISH ALUMINIUM CO. PAT. NO. DBB10
FACE TO BE POLISHED AND EDGES TO HAVE CLEAN SURFACES

A

1" ⅛"

10" ½" 1½" 1" ¼" 6½"

1½" ½"

D 1022

32 HOLES .086 DIA (NO. 44 DRILL)
CSK 1/16" DEEP FOR NO. 4 SELF TAPPING
PHILLIPS RECESS CSK HD SCREW 5/16" LG

MILD STEEL BASEPLATE
GROUND OF PLATES TO BE PAINTED
BLACK GLOSS FINISH
PLATES MARKED THUS + WHICH
WERE PAINTED 'KEMITONE'
SIGNAL RED LATTER PAINTED BLACK
WHEN RESPECTIVE LOCO'S WERE
PAINTED MAROON

1 3/4

ALUMINIUM BEADING NE 4 B.S.S. 1476
AS BRITISH ALUMINIUM CO. PAT. NO. DBB10
FACE TO BE POLISHED AND EDGES TO HAVE CLEAN SURFACES

ALUMINIUM BEADING NE 4 B.S.S. 1476
AS BRITISH ALUMINIUM CO. PAT. NO. DBB10
FACE TO BE POLISHED AND EDGES TO HAVE CLEAN SURFACES

12 CSK HOLES .191" DIA (NO. 11 DRILL)
FOR 3/16" DIA TLP/K/639 BS RIVET
'POP' RIVET
AS SUPPLIED BY TUCKER EYELET CO
OR SIMILAR

6' 7" TO RAIL LEVEL

CONSTRUCTIONAL DETAILS FOR THE MODEL MAKER
D1000 CLASS
DRILLING AND FIXING DETAIL
NUMBERPLATE
DRAWN BY: D. BIRT
DATE: 15.6.85
DRG. NO. **DB.2.**

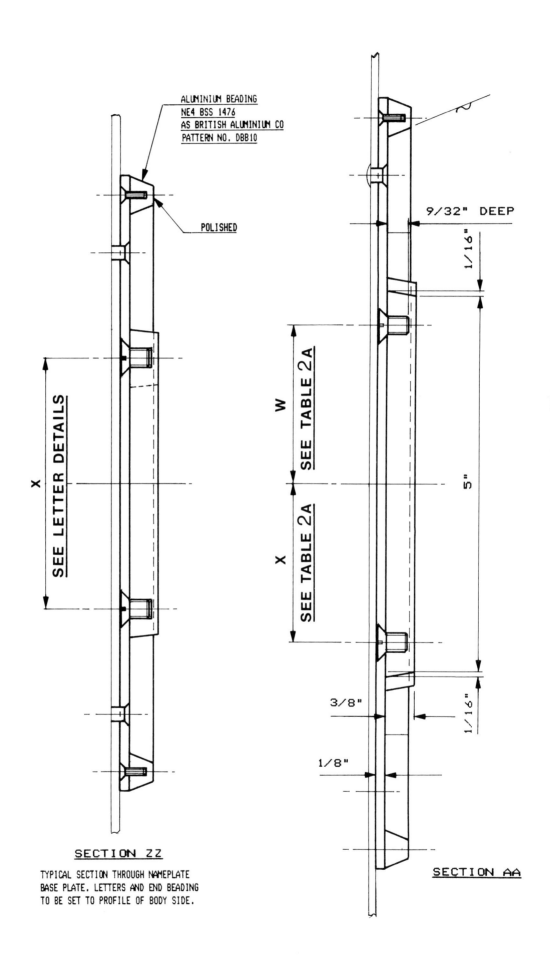

ALUMINIUM BEADING
NE4 BSS 1476
AS BRITISH ALUMINIUM CO
PATTERN NO. DBB10

POLISHED

X

SEE LETTER DETAILS

SECTION ZZ

TYPICAL SECTION THROUGH NAMEPLATE
BASE PLATE. LETTERS AND END BEADING
TO BE SET TO PROFILE OF BODY SIDE.

9/32" DEEP

1/16"

W

SEE TABLE 2A

X

SEE TABLE 2A

5"

3/8"

1/16"

1/8"

SECTION AA

Scale: = ⁴/5th Full size

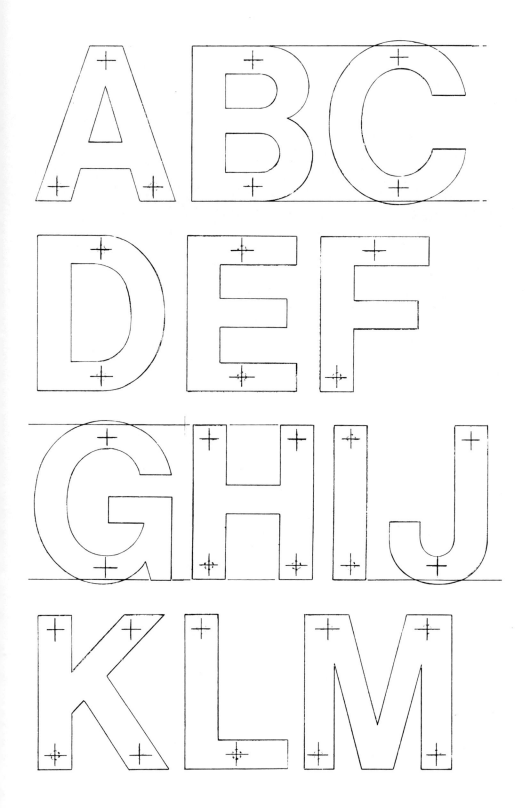

ALPHABET FOR LOCOMOTIVE NAMES

Scale: 40% Full size

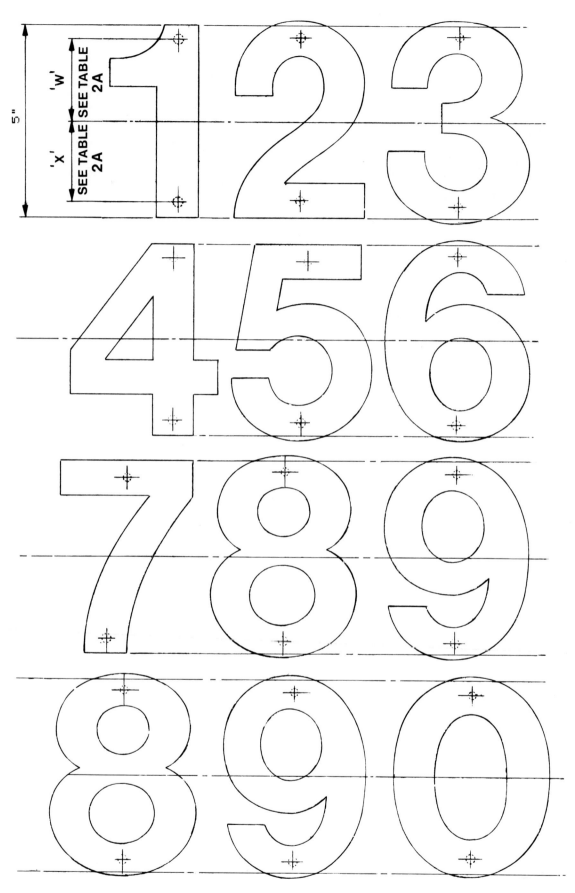

TABLE 2A										
FIG	1	2	3	4	5	6	7	8	9	0
'W'	2 1/16"		2 3/16"	2 1/16"	2"	2 3/16"	2"	2 3/16"	2 1/8"	2 1/16"
'X'	2 1/16"	2"	2 1/8"	2 1/16"	2 1/8"	2 3/16"	2 1/16"	2 1/8"	2 3/16"	2 1/16"

Letter and figures to be cast aluminium LM20 BSS1490. Faces to be polished and edges to be left with clean surface.

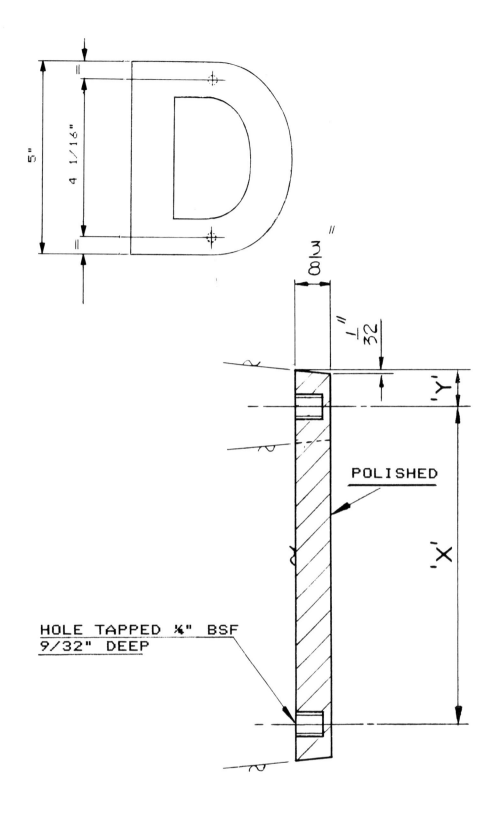

5"

4 1/16"

3/8"

1/32"

'Y'

POLISHED

'X'

HOLE TAPPED ¼" BSF
9/32" DEEP

SECTION AA

TYPICAL SECTION THROUGH
LETTER FIXING HOLES

NOTE:-

LETTERS C,G,O,Q & S   'X'=3 7/16", 'Y'=13/32"
LETTERS J & U   'X'=3 5/16", 'Y'=3/8"
FOR ALL OTHER LETTERS 'X'=3¾", 'Y'=3/8"

Letter and figure templates for
other details see section 'AA' on
example DRG DB2.
Scale: 40% Full size.

ALL LETTERS CAST ALUMINIMUM TO BSS1490 LM20

TABLE 1
DIMENSIONS BETWEEN LETTER FIXING CENTRES (SEE ALPHABET BELOW FOR DATUMS) (INCHES)

HORIZONTAL COLUMN

		A	B	C	D	E	F	G	H	I	J	K	L	M	N	O	P	Q	R	S	T	U	V	W	X	Y	Z
V	A		6	6				6 1/16		5 1/4			5 1/4	7 11/16	7 1/8				6 1/4	6	5	1	6 5/8				
E	B	5 7/8											4 13/16						5 5/8			7					
R	C	6 1/16		6 1/4		5 3/4			7 5/16	4 3/4		6 3/4				6 3/16			5 3/4		5 13/16					
T	D	5 1/2				5 3/4				4 3/4						6			5 3/4	5 7/8		7 1/8	7				6 3/8
I	E		6 1/8	5 7/8		6	6	5 3/4		5			5	7 3/4	7 3/8	5 3/4			6	5 3/8	5 3/4		7 1/8			6 5/8	
C	F					5 1/2				4 1/2			4 1/2							5 3/8	6 7/8						
A	G	6 1/4		6		6				5			5	7 1/2	6						7 3/8						
L	H	4 1/2				4 7/8	4 7/8			3 7/8												6 1/8		7 1/8			
C	I	4 3/4		4 7/8	5	5	5	5 1/4					4		6 3/8	4 7/8			5 3/16	4 7/8	4 1/2						
O	J	4 1/2																									
L	K					5 1/4				4 3/16										4 7/8							
U	L	6 5/16				6 5/8				5 5/8			5 5/8			6 1/8					5 11/16			8 11/16			
M	M	4 3/4	5 1/4							4 1/8					5 1/16	5 1/4						6 1/4					
N	N	4 3/4		5 1/8	5 1/8	5 1/8		5 1/8		3 7/8						5 1/16				5 1/8	4 3/8		5 7/8				
	O		6	6		5 7/8							7 3/4	7 1/4	6	6	6		6			7 1/8	7 1/4	8 9/16		7	
	P	4 7/8				5 1/2				4 3/8			4 3/8						5 1/4								
	Q																					7 5/8					
	R	5 13/16		6 3/8	6	5 3/4		6 7/16		5 1/4	7			7 1/4	5 3/4	6		6 3/8	6		5 7/8	7				6 5/8	
	S	5 1/2		6		5 7/8				4 7/8		6 7/8	7 3/4			6				5 1/2	5 3/8	7 1/4					
	T	5 1/4				5 1/2			6 7/8	4 1/2			4 1/2		5 5/8				5 3/4	5 3/4		6 3/4				6 1/4	
	U	4 1/2		5 3/16		5 1/8				4		6 1/8	4	6 1/2					5 1/8	4 1/2							
	V	4				4 5/8				3 15/16					4 3/4												
	W	4 1/8				4 1/2									6												
	X																4 7/8										
	Y					4 3/4																					
	Z																										

Example showing method of spacing letters
Subject: "Western Sentinel"
1. The spacings for "Western" are in all cases identical to those shown on the 7'-10 3/8" plate
2. For dimension N-S find column 'C' in Table 2 and read off dimension against "Western Sentinel" in column headed Loco Name.
3. For S-E, find S in vertical column of Table 1 and read across to E in horizontal column. Figure shown gives dimension S-E.
4. For E-N, find E in vertical column of Table 1 and read across to N in horizontal column. Figure shown gives dimension E-N.
   Similarly dimensions N-T, T-1, I-N, N-E, E-L can be found.

TABLE 1 A

LOCO NUMBER	ASSEMBLY NO. (COMP.) 2 REQD PER LOCO	DIMENSION 'Z'	DIMENSION 'Y'	LOCO NUMBER	ASSEMBLY NO. (COMP.) 2 REQD PER LOCO	DIMENSION 'Z'	DIMENSION 'Y'
D1000	3/SL/SW/3009	2' 11 1/8"	2' 7 5/8"	D1037 +	40/SL/SW/3009	2' 10 3/8"	2' 6 7/8"
D1001	4/SL/SW/3009	2' 8 3/4"	2' 5 1/4"	D1038 +	41/SL/SW/3009	2' 10 9/16"	2' 7 1/16"
D1002 +	5/SL/SW/3009	2' 10 3/8"	2' 6 7/8"	D1039	42/SL/SW/3009	2' 10 1/2"	2' 7"
D1003 +	6/SL/SW/3009	2' 10 13/16"	2' 7 5/16"	D1040	43/SL/SW/3009	2' 10 3/4"	2' 7 1/4"
D1004 +	7/SL/SW/3009	2' 10 15/16"	2' 7 7/16"	D1041	44/SL/SW/3009	2' 8 15/16"	2' 5 7/16"
D1005	8/SL/SW/3009	2' 11"	2' 7 1/2"	D1042	45/SL/SW/3009	2' 10 1/4"	2' 6 3/4"
D1006	9/SL/SW/3009	2' 11 1/8"	2' 7 5/8"	D1043	46/SL/SW/3009	2' 10 3/8"	2' 6 7/8"
D1007	10/SL/SW/3009	2' 10 1/2"	2' 7"	D1044	47/SL/SW/3009	2' 10 1/2"	2' 7"
D1008	11/SL/SW/3009	2' 11 1/8"	2' 7 5/8"	D1045	48/SL/SW/3009	2' 10 3/8"	2' 6 7/8"
D1009	12/SL/SW/3009	2' 11 1/16"	2' 7 9/16"	D1046	49/SL/SW/3009	2' 10 1/2"	2' 7"
D1010	13/SL/SW/3009	2' 8 7/8"	2' 5 3/8"	D1047	50/SL/SW/3009	2' 10 1/8"	2' 6 5/8"
D1011	14/SL/SW/3009	2' 6 7/8"	2' 3 3/8"	D1048	51/SL/SW/3009	2' 10 9/16"	2' 7 1/16"
D1012	15/SL/SW/3009	2' 8 1/16"	2' 4 9/16"	D1049	52/SL/SW/3009	2' 10 3/8"	2' 6 7/8"
D1013	16/SL/SW/3009	2' 8 3/8"	2' 4 7/8"	D1050	53/SL/SW/3009	2' 10 11/16"	2' 7 3/16"
D1014	17/SL/SW/3009	2' 8 9/16"	2' 5 1/16"	D1051	54/SL/SW/3009	2' 8 7/8"	2' 5 3/8"
D1015	18/SL/SW/3009	2' 8 5/16"	2' 4 13/16"	D1052	55/SL/SW/3009	2' 10 1/8"	2' 6 5/8"
D1016	19/SL/SW/3009	2' 8 5/8"	2' 5 1/8"	D1053	56/SL/SW/3009	2' 10 5/16	2' 6 13/16"
D1017	20/SL/SW/3009	2' 8 1/16"	2' 4 9/16"	D1054	57/SL/SW/3009	2' 10 7/16"	2' 6 15/16"
D1018	21/SL/SW/3009	2' 8 1/2"	2' 5"	D1055	58/SL/SW/3009	2' 10 3/8"	2' 6 7/8"
D1019	22/SL/SW/3009	2' 8 5/16"	2' 4 13/16"	D1056	59/SL/SW/3009	2' 10 1/2"	2' 7"
D1020	23/SL/SW/3009	2' 10 3/16"	2' 6 11/16"	D1057	60/SL/SW/3009	2' 10 1/8"	2' 6 5/8"
D1021	24/SL/SW/3009	2' 8 1/2"	2' 5"	D1058	61/SL/SW/3010	2' 10 5/8"	2' 7 1/8"
D1022	25/SL/SW/3009	2' 9 3/4"	2' 6 1/4"	D1059	62/SL/SW/3009	2' 10 1/2"	2' 7"
D1023	26/SL/SW/3009	2' 9 7/8"	2' 6 3/8"	D1060	63/SL/SW/3009	2' 11"	2' 7 1/2"
D1024	27/SL/SW/3009	2' 10"	2' 6 1/2"	D1061	64/SL/SW/3009	2' 9 1/16"	2' 5 9/16"
D1025	28/SL/SW/3009	2' 9 13/16"	2' 6 5/16"	D1062	65/SL/SW/3009	2' 10 3/8"	2' 6 7/8"
D1026	29/SL/SW/3009	2' 9 15/16"	2' 6 7/16"	D1063	66/SL/SW/3009	2' 10 5/8"	2' 7 1/8"
D1027	30/SL/SW/3009	2' 9 5/8"	2' 6 1/8"	D1064	67/SL/SW/3009	2' 10 3/4"	2' 7 1/4"
D1028	31/SL/SW/3009	2' 10 1/16"	2' 6 9/16"	D1065	68/SL/SW/3009	2' 10 9/16"	2' 7 1/16"
D1029	32/SL/SW/3009	2' 10"	2' 6 1/2"	D1066	69/SL/SW/3009	2' 10 11/16"	2' 7 3/16"
D1030	33/SL/SW/3009	2' 10 11/16"	2' 7 3/16"	D1067	70/SL/SW/3009	2' 10 3/8"	2' 6 7/8"
D1031	34/SL/SW/3009	2' 8 3/4"	2' 5 1/4"	D1068	71/SL/SW/3009	2' 10 3/4"	2' 7 1/4"
D1032	35/SL/SW/3009	2' 9 15/16"	2' 6 7/16"	D1069	72/SL/SW/3009	2' 10 9/16"	2' 7 1/16"
D1033	36/SL/SW/3009	2' 10 1/4"	2' 6 3/4"	D1070	73/SL/SW/3009	2' 10 1/8"	2' 6 5/8"
D1034	37/SL/SW/3009	2' 10 5/16"	2' 6 13/16"	D1071	74/SL/SW/3009	2' 8 7/16"	2' 4 15/16"
D1035 +	38/SL/SW/3009	2' 10 1/2"	2' 7"	D1072	75/SL/SW/3009	2' 9 11/16"	2' 6 3/16"
D1036 +	39/SL/SW/3009	2' 10 9/16"	2' 7 1/16"	D1073	76/SL/SW/3009	2' 9 13/16"	2' 6 5/16"

Mild steel baseplates.

Ground of plates painted black gloss finish.

Plates marked thus + were 'Kemitone' signal red and were painted black when respective locomotives received the maroon livery.

TABLE 2

LOCO NO.	LOCO NAME	A	B	C	1/4" DIA BSF CSK HEAD SCREW 3/8" LONG BSS 450	NO. 4 PHILLIPS RECESS CSK HD SELF TAPPING SCREW 5/16" LONG	3/16" DIA TLP/K/ 639 BS RIVET	ASSEMBLY NO. (COMP.) 2 REQD PER LOCO
D1001	WESTERN PATHFINDER	8'9"	8'5 1/2"	8 3/4"	45	54	42	2/SL/SW/2932
D1002 +	WESTERN EXPLORER	7'11 3/8"	7'7 7/8"	8 3/4"	39	50	38	3/SL/SW/2932
D1003 +	WESTERN PIONEER	7'5 1/4"	7'1 3/4"	8 3/4"	36	46	34	4/SL/SW/2932
D1004 +	WESTERN CRUSADER	8'0 5/8"	7'9 1/8"	9 1/8"	39	50	38	5/SL/SW/2932
D1005	WESTERN VENTURER	8'0 5/8"	7'9 1/8"	9 3/4"	39	50	38	6/SL/SW/2932
D1006	WESTERN STALWART	7'11 7/8"	7' 8 3/8"	8 3/8"	39	50	38	7/SL/SW/2932
D1007	WESTERN TALISMAN	7'11 3/8"	7'7 7/8"	9"	41	50	38	8/SL/SW/2932
D1008	WESTERN HARRIER	7'5 7/8"	7'2 3/8"	10"	39	46	34	9/SL/SW/2932
D1009	WESTERN INVADER	7'4 5/8"	7'1 1/8"	7 3/4"	38	46	34	10/SL/SW/2932
D1010	WESTERN CAMPAIGNER	9'1"	8'9 1/2"	9 1/8"	46	54	42	11/SL/SW/2932
D1011	WESTERN THUNDERER	8'8"	8'4 1/2"	9"	44	54	42	12/SL/SW/2932
D1012	WESTERN FIREBRAND	8'4 3/4"	8' 1 1/4"	8 3/4"	42	50	38	13/SL/SW/2932
D1013	WESTERN RANGER	7'1 3/4"	6'10 1/4"	8 3/4"	36	46	30	14/SL/SW/2932
D1014	WESTERN LEVIATHAN	8'3 1/4"	7'11 3/4"	7 3/4"	44	50	38	15/SL/SW/2932
D1015	WESTERN CHAMPION	7'11 7/8"	7'8 3/8"	9 1/8"	42	50	38	16/SL/SW/2932
D1016	WESTERN GLADIATOR	8'3 1/2"	8'0"	9 1/8"	40	50	38	17/SL/SW/2932
D1017	WESTERN WARRIOR	7'6 1/2"	7'3"	11 1/8"	39	46	34	18/SL/SW/2932
D1018	WESTERN BUCCANEER	8'8 3/8"	8'4 7/8"	8 3/4"	42	54	42	19/SL/SW/2932
D1019	WESTERN CHALLENGER	9'1 7/8"	8'10 3/8"	9 1/8"	45	54	42	20/SL/SW/2932
D1020	WESTERN HERO	6'1 5/8"	5'10 1/8"	10"	30	42	26	21/SL/SW/2932
D1021	WESTERN CAVALIER	7'10 5/8"	7'7 1/8"	9 1/8"	39	50	38	22/SL/SW/2932
D1022	WESTERN SENTINEL	7'10 3/8"	7'6 7/8"	8 3/8"	39	50	38	23/SL/SW/2932
D1023	WESTERN FUSILIER	7'8 1/2"	7'5"	8 3/4"	37	50	38	24/SL/SW/2932
D1024	WESTERN HUNTSMAN	8'1 7/8"	7'10 3/8"	10"	45	50	38	25/SL/SW/2932
D1025	WESTERN GUARDSMAN	8'8 1/4"	8'4 3/4"	9 1/8"	45	54	42	26/SL/SW/2932
D1026	WESTERN CENTURION	8'5 3/8"	8'1 7/8"	9 1/8"	43	50	38	27/SL/SW/2932
D1027	WESTERN LANCER	7'1"	6'9 1/2"	7 3/4"	35	46	30	28/SL/SW/2932
D1028	WESTERN HUSSAR	7'0 3/4"	6'9 1/4"	10"	36	46	30	29/SL/SW/2932
D1029	WESTERN LEGIONAIRE	8'9 1/4"	8'5 3/4"	7 3/4"	43	54	42	30/SL/SW/2932
D1030	WESTERN MUSKETEER	8'7 5/8"	8'4 1/8"	10 5/8"	43	50	38	31/SL/SW/2932
D1031	WESTERN RIFLEMAN	7'11 1/4"	7'7 3/4"	8 3/4"	41	50	38	32/SL/SW/2932
D1032	WESTERN MARKSMAN	8'2 5/8"	7'11 1/8"	10 5/8"	46	50	38	33/SL/SW/2932
D1033	WESTERN TROOPER	7'6 7/8"	7'3 3/8"	9"	35	46	34	34/SL/SW/2932
D1034	WESTERN DRAGOON	7'7 3/8"	7'3 7/8"	9"	37	46	34	35/SL/SW/2932
D1035 +	WESTERN YEOMAN	7'1"	6'9 1/2"	9 3/8"	37	46	30	36/SL/SW/2932
D1036 +	WESTERN EMPEROR	7'7 7/8"	7'4 3/8"	8 3/4"	37	46	34	37/SL/SW/2932
D1037 +	WESTERN EMPRESS	7'6 3/8"	7'2 7/8"	8 3/4"	36	46	34	38/SL/SW/2932
D1038 +	WESTERN SOVEREIGN	8'5 3/8"	8'1 7/8"	8 3/8"	41	50	38	39/SL/SW/2932
D1039	WESTERN KING	6'0 1/2"	5'9"	9 3/4"	31	38	26	40/SL/SW/2932
D1040	WESTERN QUEEN	6'8 3/4"	6'5 1/4"	9 1/8"	32	46	30	41/SL/SW/2932
D1041	WESTERN PRINCE	6'11 1/2"	6'8"	8 3/4"	34	46	30	42/SL/SW/2932
D1042	WESTERN PRINCESS	7'10 1/4"	7'6 3/4"	8 3/4"	38	50	38	43/SL/SW/2932
D1043	WESTERN DUKE	6'2 1/2"	5'11"	9"	30	42	26	44/SL/SW/2932
D1044	WESTERN DUCHESS	7'7 1/4"	7'3 3/4"	9"	36	46	34	45/SL/SW/2932
D1045	WESTERN VISCOUNT	7'11 5/8"	7'8 1/8"	9 3/4"	39	50	38	46/SL/SW/2932
D1046	WESTERN MARQUIS	7'7 5/8"	7'4 1/8"	10 5/8"	38	46	34	47/SL/SW/2932
D1047	WESTERN LORD	6'0 5/8"	5'9 1/8"	7 3/4"	28	38	26	48/SL/SW/2932
D1048	WESTERN LADY	6'0 1/4"	5'8 3/4"	7 3/4"	29	38	26	49/SL/SW/2932
D1049	WESTERN MONARCH	7'9 1/8"	7'5 5/8"	10 5/8"	41	50	38	50/SL/SW/2932
D1050	WESTERN RULER	6'7 1/4"	6'3 3/4"	8 3/4"	32	42	30	51/SL/SW/2932
D1051	WESTERN AMBASSADOR	9'1 3/8"	8'9 7/8"	8 5/8"	45	54	42	52/SL/SW/2932
D1052	WESTERN VICEROY	7'4 7/8"	7'1 3/8"	9 3/4"	36	46	34	53/SL/SW/2932
D1053	WESTERN PATRIARCH	8'3 7/8"	8'0 3/8"	8 3/4"	43	50	38	54/SL/SW/2932
D1054	WESTERN GOVERNOR	8' 2 1/4"	7'10 3/4"	9 1/8"	40	50	38	55/SL/SW/2932
D1055	WESTERN ADVOCATE	8'0"	7'8 1/2"	8 5/8"	38	50	38	56/SL/SW/2932
D1056	WESTERN SULTAN	6'11 1/4"	6'7 3/4"	8 3/8"	35	46	30	57/SL/SW/2932
D1057	WESTERN CHIEFTAIN	8' 3 1/8"	7'11 5/8"	9 1/8"	42	50	38	58/SL/SW/2932
D1058	WESTERN NOBLEMAN	8'0 1/2"	7'9"	9 1/2"	42	50	38	59/SL/SW/2932
D1059	WESTERN EMPIRE	7'0"	6'8 1/2"	8 3/4"	34	46	30	60/SL/SW/2932
D1060	WESTERN DOMINION	7'10 3/4"	7' 7 1/4"	9"	41	50	38	61/SL/SW/2932
D1061	WESTERN ENVOY	6'7 1/2"	6'4"	8 3/4"	33	42	30	62/SL/SW/2932
D1062	WESTERN COURIER	7'6 3/4"	7'3 1/4"	9 1/8"	36	46	34	63/SL/SW/2932
D1063	WESTERN MONITOR	7'5 7/8"	7' 2 3/8"	10 5/8"	38	46	34	64/SL/SW/2932
D1064	WESTERN REGENT	7'0 5/8"	6'9 1/8"	8 3/4"	34	46	30	65/SL/SW/2932
D1065	WESTERN CONSORT	7'8 1/4"	7'4 3/4"	9 1/8"	36	50	38	66/SL/SW/2932
D1066	WESTERN PREFECT	7'5 5/8"	7'2 1/8"	8 3/4"	34	46	34	67/SL/SW/2932
D1067	WESTERN DRUID	6'5 1/2"	6'2"	9"	31	42	30	68/SL/SW/2932
D1068	WESTERN RELIANCE	7'10 7/8"	7'7 3/8"	8 3/4"	39	50	38	69/SL/SW/2932
D1069	WESTERN VANGUARD	8'0 7/8"	7'9 3/8"	9 3/4"	42	50	38	70/SL/SW/2932
D1070	WESTERN GAUNTLET	8'0 3/4"	7'9 1/4"	9 1/8"	39	50	38	71/SL/SW/2932
D1071	WESTERN RENOWN	7'3"	6'11 1/2"	8 3/4"	38	46	34	72/SL/SW/2932
D1072	WESTERN GLORY	6'6 5/8"	6'3 1/8"	9 1/8"	31	42	30	73/SL/SW/2932
D1073	WESTERN BULWARK	7'7 3/4"	7'4 1/4"	8 3/4"	40	46	34	74/SL/SW/2932

		TABLE 3								
		HORIZONTAL COLUMN								
		1	2	3	4	5	6	7	8	9	0

V E R T I C A L C O L U M N		1	2	3	4	5	6	7	8	9	0
	1	4 1/4"	4 1/4"	4 3/8"	5 1/4"	4 7/16"	4 5/8"	4 3/16"	4 7/16"	4 5/16"	4 11/16"
	2	5 7/16"	5 1/2"	5 1/2"	6 1/4"	5 1/2"	5 7/16"	5 5/16"	5 9/16"	5 9/16"	5 9/16"
	3	5 3/8"	5 3/8"	5 1/2"	6 1/4"	5 13/16"	5 13/16"	5 13/16"	5 13/16"	5 3/4"	5 3/4"
	4	4 3/4"	4 7/8"	4 7/8"	5 5/8"	5	4 7/8"	4 11/16"	4 15/16"	4 13/16"	5"
	5	5 5/16"	5 3/8"	5 7/16"	6 3/16"	5 9/16"	5 1/2"	5 5/16"	5 5/8"	5 9/16"	5 9/16"
	6	5 1/2"	5 5/8"	5 11/16"	6 1/2"	5 13/16"	5 3/4"	5 9/16"	5 3/4"	5 5/8"	5 7/8"
	7	5 5/16"	5 3/8"	5 3/8"							5 7/16"
	8										
	9					6"					
	0	5 3/16"	5 5/8"	5 15/16"	6 3/4"	6 1/8"	6 1/8"	5 11/16"	6 1/8"	6 1/8"	6 1/8"

Example for locomotive No. D1022 working from left to right
1. Dimension D-1 see example Drg. DB.1.
2. For 1-0, find 1 in vertical column, read to 0 horizontal column and figure gives dimension between fixing centres.
3. For 0-2, find 0 in vertical column, read across to 2 in horizontal column and figure gives dimension between fixing centres.
4. For 2-2, find 2 in vertical column, read across to 2 in horizontal column and figure gives dimension between fixing centres.

D1058 Western Nobleman
showing the cast number plat
with data panel beneath.

The cast nameplate of a 'Western
– held at 38 points!

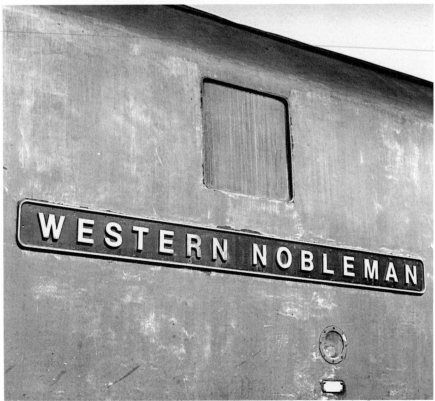

D1041 at Crewe 2nd July 198.
with D5054 beyond.

Westerns Preserved

Locomotive	Ownership	Under the care of	Notes
D1010 Western Campaigner	Foster Yeoman Ltd Torr Works East Cranmore Shepton Mallet Somerset	Diesel & Electric Group c/o Great Western Railway Society, Didcot, Oxon.	
D1013 Western Ranger	Richard Holdsworth Conversions Ltd London Bridge Rd Woodley, Reading, Berks	Western Locomotive Association, c/o Severn Valley Railway Co. Ltd, Bewdley, Worcs.	
D1015 Western Champion	The Diesel Traction Group	BREL Swindon, Wilts.	
D1023 Western Fusilier	National Railway Museum Leeman Road York	On Loan To: Dart Valley Railway, Devon.	
D1041 Western Prince	Privately Owned By: D.H. Edleston Osmaston Park Rd Derby	East Lancashire Railway Bury, Lancs.	
D1048 Western Lady	D1048 Western Lady Ltd	Steamport Southport, Merseyside.	Formerly owned by:- D. Rigby, Blackrod, Near Bolton, Lancs, and was under the care of NYMR.
D1062 Western Courier	Western Locomotive Association	Severn Valley Railway Co. Ltd, Bewdley, Worcs.	

D1023 Western Fusilier undergoes restoration at the National Railway Museum, York.
(Crown Copyright, NRM)

D1041 Western Prince at the Crewe 150th anniversary celebrations, 2nd July 1987 with owner Mr. D. H. Edleston.

D1023 Western Fusilier having undergone its repaint at the N.R.M. Seen here in its original magnificence of maroon livery.

Western Acknowledgements

I would like to thank the following for the kind help given to me in the preparation of this book, without whose help the work would not have been possible.

Members of the Staff at British Rail Laira Depot.
Members of the Staff at British Rail Old Oak Common Depot.
Drivers based at Westbury Depot.
TOPS of Bristol for information regarding the log of D1022.
The General Works Manager of British Rail Engineering Ltd, Swindon Works.
National Railway Museum, York.
Richard Holdsworth, for information regarding D1013 *Western Ranger*.
Driver F. J. Boase of Laira.
Foster Yeoman Ltd, of Shepton Mallet, Somerset.
Mr. George Russam of the Western Locomotive Association.
Mr. J. E. Buckland, Mr. Steve Crowther, Mr. Chris Guntripp and Mr. G. Toms.
Special thanks to Mr. D. H. Edleston for his kind co-operation and enthusiasm for this work.
Mr. W. E. Gray, Senior Lecturer, Blackpool College of Higher Education.
Mr. Millroy, Shed Foreman, Tyseley Depot.
Russell Carter for drawings.
British Rail Personnel, BREL Crewe Works.
To Hazel Glover, for her professionalism and kind assistance in typing of the final manuscript and with a special thanks to Diane, for her loyalty and devotion in the typing of the initial scripts which subsequently led to the materialisation of this work.

Finally to W.J. Campbell for his most kind and valuable assistance.

Picture Credits

David Birt ARPS (All photographs and drawings unless otherwise stated)
National Railway Museum (Crown Copyright)
British Rail
Mr. K. Collier
Mr. S. Crowther
Mr. G. F. Gillham
Mr. C. Guntripp
Mr. M. Mensing
Mr. R. C. H. Nash
Mr. P. D. Nicholson
Mr. N. E. Preedy

Bibliography

Modern Railways (1960-1974) Ian Allan
Railway World (1960-1974) Ian Allan
Railway Magazine (1960-1974) IPC Transport Press
Western Enterprise – British Rail Western, London Division
Western Stock List – Steam and Diesel Publications
Western Anthology – Peter Watts
Western Memories – Peter Watts
Diesel Railway Traction (March 62) – British Rail
Rail News – British Rail, London
Rail Enthusiast – EMAP National Publications
Standard Gauge Times – Railway Times (NGE)
Profile of the Westerns – OPC
The Power of the Westerns – OPC

New Year's day 1977 at Westbury
Depot. D1010 Western Cam-
paigner is the only member of the
class to be seen. A sad reminder
of their closing days.

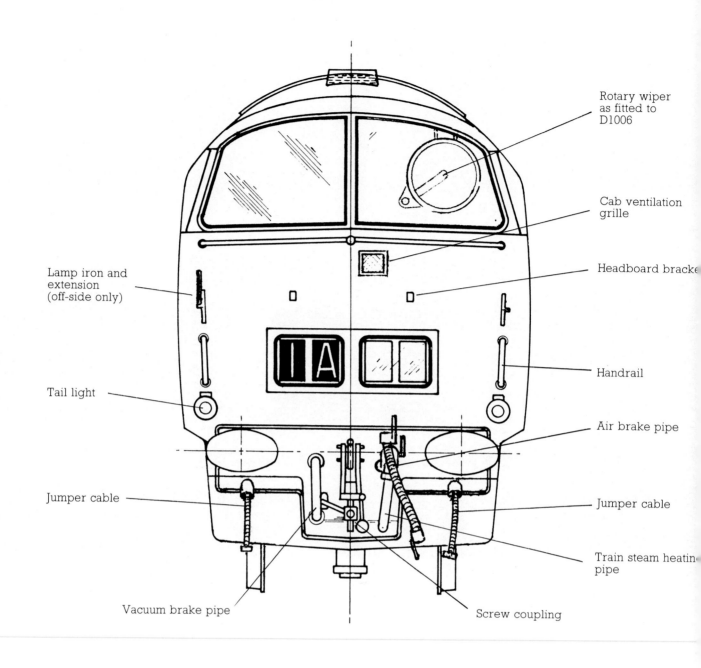

Rotary wiper
as fitted to
D1006

Cab ventilation
grille

Headboard bracke

Lamp iron and
extension
(off-side only)

Handrail

Tail light

Air brake pipe

Jumper cable

Jumper cable

Train steam heatin
pipe

Vacuum brake pipe

Screw coupling

The End